Challenge Your Assumptions Change Your World

Introducing the Assumpt! A Breakthrough to Faster, Better Business Decisions

ANDY COHEN

D1472250

Challenge Your Assumptions, Change Your World
Copyright 2016 © Andy Cohen

1Astor Place Publishing

Paperback ISBN: 978-1629670768

Cover Design: Julia Gang
Interior Design: Robin Krauss

Patience is a necessary requirement of writing that is unfairly thrust upon those closest to the author. This book is dedicated to my loving wife, Deborah, who watched this book evolve, dissolve, and be rebuilt and stood by me all the way. You are a Saint.

TABLE OF CONTENTS

PART 1

How Understanding Your Assumptions Makes Your Life Better

Let's start with the good news: You already know how to make assumptions. They are a natural component in your daily decision-making process, and you've been making them your whole life. The bad news is you've been taught "you shouldn't assume," which contradicts and undermines the assumption's role in making smarter, better decisions. Attempting to avoid making assumptions is as impossible as trying to stop breathing. It can't be done. Instead, you can learn to utilize your assumptions productively and in ways you haven't imagined.

But how do you identify your assumptions? How do you separate out those that help or hurt? Build or destroy? Solve problems or create new ones? The pages that follow offer pathways for identifying, managing, and challenging your assumptions in ways that provide you the power to enhance your career and, as you will discover, truly change your world.

CHAPTER 1

How This Book Can Help You

This book is about seeing things for what they are, or are not, so you can always make the best decision under any circumstance. More specifically, it is about ideas, choices, opportunities, and solutions and how to get more of the right ones to drive your success in business and in life.

Consider this book a journey that equips you with more arrows in your mental quiver. You will have more options to draw from when faced with change or what feels like insurmountable odds. Your arrows will be not only plentiful but also constructed in a way that lets you clearly take aim and increase the odds of hitting the bull's-eye with greater accuracy. This journey enhances your ability to overcome the perceived barriers keeping you from achieving your daily goals and long-term dreams. You'll discover the infinite rewards of challenging your assumptions, which include creating the opportunities you seek.

In writing this book I picture you, the reader, as someone who is smart and has tasted success more than a few times. So why, then, do you need to augment your thinking?

There are three reasons:

1) **As Einstein said, "We cannot solve our problems with the same level of thinking that created them."** In today's

competitive atmosphere, you are tossed more and more problems at work as the pace of change intensifies. Using the same bat as before to hit them no longer works. You need ways to think differently to manage these changes. This book will offer tools to uncover different bats, adapt your stance, and shift your thinking.

2) **As Benjamin Franklin said, "If everyone is thinking alike, then no one is thinking."** People in the same industry read the same websites, talk the same language, and follow the same trends. They end up thinking just like each other. The same is true within organizations that share the same corporate speak, follow the same rules, and embrace similar beliefs. Thinking and acting differently is the ability to break free of the traditional way of responding or doing something and explore what you or your peers consider "impossible" or "improbable"—or, in corporate speak, breaking free of the phrase, "That's not the way we do things around here."

Don't fool yourself into thinking that doing things differently requires having the "guts" to break from the crowd or take significant risks. It's so much simpler. You just need a way to see the multiple paths that others don't see and then show them how to follow those paths.

But how do you see these invisible paths? And what do you do when you come upon them? Do you choose just one or all? This book gives you a road map to help lead your exploration. The first step you need to take is to reexplore your assumption about assumptions.

3) **The head of a Hollywood film studio once said, "Assumptions are the mother of all screw-ups."**[1] He actually used a more descriptive and coarser word than "screw-up," but I think you get the point.

But what if I suggested this isn't true? Yes, we all make assumptions we treat as facts even though they are just beliefs, and upon occasion, those assumptions mess things up with our peers, clients, family, and friends. However, the truth is your assumptions are neither good nor bad. They are important steps in your decision-making process, and contrary to what you might think, you make them all the time.

As we will discuss later, assumptions are one of the rungs of the ladder in your decision-making process. You use them as shortcuts. When you sit in a chair, you assume it will hold you. There is no need to test it. When you eat at a restaurant, you assume the food is okay to eat. You don't go into the kitchen to see how it's being cooked (though maybe you should in some establishments). When you say something to someone, you generally assume the person understands; you don't bombard him or her with a million questions to verify comprehension. When you make a mobile-to-mobile payment, you assume it's safe and press the send button without thought. When you create a business plan, you assume a number of things that can only be tested after the plan is executed.

In other words, assumptions serve an important function in processing your decisions and determining your actions. If you had to question every single thing you take for granted, you couldn't operate in this world. Nothing would move.

The reality that you make assumptions all the time isn't an issue. It's how you identify and then manage your assumptions that makes a difference in your outcomes.

Those who recognize their assumptions and then challenge them are the ones who drive new solutions. For example, it's easy to assume that if you make your product or service better, it will fend off the competition. But often that kind of assumption leaves you looking inward at what you do best rather than outward as to what the customer really wants. That's the assumption Blockbuster made as Netflix entered the DVD marketplace. Blockbuster assumed that if it made the brick-and-mortar experience better, it would continue to own the DVD marketplace. Netflix challenged assumptions about the traditional DVD rental market and instead focused on the consumer's growing demands for more control over the DVD experience.

For example, Netflix's offer of no late fees turned customers into overnight brand advocates and left Blockbuster looking like the brand loser. Then, Netflix challenged the traditional DVD distribution system by offering customers the ability to stream videos. This put Blockbuster out of business.

With Blockbuster out of the way, Netflix continued challenging traditional industry assumptions. The company rejected the assumption that it was just a distributor of curated content and invested in providing original content with its first Emmy Award-winning *House of Cards* in 2013. Historically, TV series episodes were released on a weekly basis as a way to retain viewers. Netflix, however, made the decision to challenge the assumption behind this approach by also releasing the complete season of *House of Cards* so people could "binge-watch" as many episodes as they'd like.

Netflix was founded in 1997 as a US-based snail-mail DVD service but in less than twenty years has evolved into an international tech entertainment service in over 190 countries,[2] earning $1.8 billion in revenue as of Q1 2016.[3] Netflix revolutionized how we watch and interact with entertainment by continuing to challenge industry assumptions.

We are going to spend a lot of time on this point and how you manage your personal assumptions because making smarter decisions comes from your ability to innovate, bringing you closer to your own needs and the needs of those around you. Having the insights and tools to spot your daily assumptions and then challenge them is a crucial step in how you approach creating a start-up, building a team, strengthening your relationships, winning new business, and confronting the growing list of insurmountable and often-perceived impossible problems that plague all of us everyday.

What you will learn in this book will provide more options and a greater number of solutions because you will use your assumptions differently than ever before.

I hope this sounds appealing to you. If so, let's get to work.

CHAPTER 2

What You Fear and Love About Assumptions

Your assumption is like fire. Depending on how you use it, it can burn down your house, leaving you homeless, or it can cook your food, giving you energy. If you only invest in the negative side of fire because of a fear of the flame, you miss out on the multiple benefits that flame provides. How often do you think of your assumptions as something bad to avoid making? In this chapter, you will discover that we share a learned bias toward assumptions that constricts our ability to use them to our advantage. Luckily, overriding the maxim "I shouldn't assume" is easier than you think and is the first step toward putting your assumptions to work for you.

Dangerous Assumptions Travel Far

In the winter of 1998, NASA launched a revolutionary new spacecraft. Nine months later, it disappeared—a victim of an unforgivable assumption.

NASA had collaborated with Lockheed Martin to build the $193.1 million Mars Climate Orbiter, a robotic probe designed to orbit Mars in order to study the Martian climate, atmosphere, and surface.[1] The 745-pound machine would give the world an unprecedented glimpse at Earth's nearest planetary neighbor.[2] It signaled a natural shift in

NASA's focus: first we landed on the Moon, and now our sights were set on the mysterious red planet.

The device left Earth in December 1998 bound for Mars. It sped through space for nine months, and sky watchers both professional and amateur eagerly awaited the Orbiter's arrival at Mars. The possibilities were limitless—what would this probe uncover?

But on September 23, 1999, NASA lost contact with the probe. Upon entry into the Martian atmosphere, the craft simply disintegrated. No one could figure out why.

Soon after, an investigation revealed the culprit. The NASA engineers had used software based on the widespread metric unit of measurement, but the Lockheed Martin engineers had done their calculations for the hardware using the English unit of measurement.

The result? Catastrophe. Instead of orbiting around the planet at a safe distance, the thrusters of the Orbiter miscalculated due to the conflicting measurement units. This shot the spacecraft into the Mars atmosphere and dangerously close to its surface.

Despite months of building, full cooperation between two huge corporate and government entities, and over $327 million in total expenses,[3] the probe burned up because both sides assumed the other guy was using the same kind of ruler.

Dangerous Assumptions Can Be Found
Close to Home, Too

An assumption is something you treat as a fact, rather than a belief. It's often subconscious and therefore taken for granted. Assumptions are integrated in everything you do—whether programming software, planning your day or a meeting, designing a strategy, or starting up a company or a new family. As mentioned earlier, assumptions are neither good nor bad as they serve an important function in your decision-making process.

For instance, I play tennis early Wednesday mornings and love biking over to the courts. When it rains, I am forced to take a less enjoyable form of transportation. On these days, it feels like it rains all the time on Wednesdays. Chances are, however, that if I mark the weather conditions on a calendar, it would prove that over 80 percent of the time the weather is fine. I just remember the bad days.

The perception of making assumptions is the same. You tend not to notice all the ones you make until something goes wrong; you miscalculate the time it takes to get to a meeting, judge someone unfairly, price yourself out of a potential piece of business, say something that alienates a fellow worker, or discover that you're using a different form of measurement than your project partner. All of a sudden, the penalty for following an assumption blindly can be quite costly with ramifications that have a very long reach—sometimes as far as thirty-three million miles.

Given the range of severity and consequences in following our assumptions, it's not surprising we view them as extremely dangerous.

The Side of Assumptions You Love

But there is another side of the assumption that fascinates us and provides inner pleasure: when we see what happens when our assumptions are turned inside out and around. The artist Pablo Picasso, for example, used Cubism as a way to help us see the world differently. In his famous work *Three Musicians,* he used abstract forms to shape the players in such an unexpected way that when you first see this artwork, you assume that nothing makes sense. Yet when you look at the painting a second time, the figures come together.

Picasso's work challenges your assumptions about how space and objects are used. His artwork helps you see the world differently and reminds you there are alternative ways of using shape, objects, and colors. The reward for this is the intrinsic pleasure you get by looking at this work.

The same reward applies to the accomplishments of our historical and contemporary heroes.

We admire President John F. Kennedy for making a dream into a reality by putting a man on the Moon. Today, business entrepreneur Elon Musk is admired for putting the first successful nonmanned commercial flight into outer space, a feat many assumed would never happen in their lifetime. And he continues to make us question the impossible as his company SpaceX is looking to put a colony of eighty thousand humans[4] on Mars by 2040.[5]

Back on earth, we admire a number of thought leaders who stimulate our thinking by their contrarian viewpoints on the way we behave.

Malcolm Gladwell (*The Tipping Point, Outliers*) writes best sellers that brilliantly weave together interesting stories with equally interesting research in a way that makes you think differently by challenging your assumptions. Authors like Daniel Kahneman (*Thinking, Fast and Slow*) and Dan Ariely (*Predictably Irrational*) are masters at creating and interpreting psychological research that challenges your fundamental beliefs on how you think, make decisions, and behave. Charles Duhigg (*The Power of Habit*) and Daniel H. Pink (*Drive*) reorder your thinking processes in order to alter your behavior and motivation.

These books help you see yourself and others in a different light. They provide lessons that help you better navigate your world. Yet, as much as you enjoy having your assumptions challenged by others, you are often reluctant to actively challenge your own on a daily basis.

The barriers standing in your way are associated with those times your assumptions have backfired, putting you in an uncomfortable position or causing painful damage. These negative associations leave you saying, "I shouldn't assume," which you will soon discover is absurd.

Ever since you were little, you have been told, "Do not make assumptions." And later in life, you may have heard the expression, "To assume is to make an Ass out of U and Me."

This popular saying is rumored to have originated from Oscar Wilde. Then, legend has it that a typewriter repairman uttered it to a TV writer who brought it to national attention by integrating it into an episode of *The Odd Couple*, the hit show based on the Neil Simon play of the same name. In the episode titled "My Strife in Court," fastidious Felix defends himself in front of a judge and jury. While acting as his own attorney, he questions a witness and gets her to admit that she assumed a crucial piece of evidence.

"Did you say you assumed?" Felix shouts at the witness. Felix then pulls out a chalkboard to illustrate his point. "You should never assume," he says while drawing the word on the board. "Because when you ASSUME, you make an ASS of U and ME!"[6] Felix wins his case, and the assumption "I shall not assume" lives on.

Scientists or economists trained in the value of making assumptions to formulate a hypothesis still see their personal assumptions as "something to avoid." After I gave a lecture on this topic, a participant confided in me that she had an overwhelming fear of attending my talk because she assumed I was going to make her feel "stupid" for making assumptions. Then she added, "I am really relieved that it's okay to do."

Denying that you make assumptions keeps you from the very thing that excites you and stimulates your thinking: challenging them.

The ability to challenge and manage your assumptions makes

you the author of your own "best-selling" stories about avoiding catastrophes and creating life-changing opportunities by thinking differently. Your material is unlimited—create a new app, close an impossible sale, find the job that rewards you in satisfaction as well as pay, implement your breakthrough strategy, or develop an award-winning marketing campaign.

While you are learning to manage your own assumptions, you will also help others to manage theirs. That's why your "story" will include helping your organization, other leaders, and your peers in a manner that generates alignment, increases profits, and leads to change.

The following chapters will break down those childhood prejudices about making assumptions and then provide a practical way to help you use your assumptions to your advantage. This is one of the key takeaways that make this book different—that you should embrace your assumptions rather than judge yourself for making them. Embracing them gives you the power to manage them in ways that lead to better decisions. Judging yourself for making them undermines that purpose. As a result, your assumptions manage you, limiting your decision-making capabilities. Mastering your assumptions does the opposite.

CHAPTER 3

Why Your Assumptions
Are neither Good nor Bad

You're on a roll at work. Everything is going your way. You feel great. Then, someone or something spoils it. Like most of us, you look around for someone to blame.

But suppose the problem is you? If that's the case, it's a good thing because it means you are the one who is actually in control of the situation, and you have the power to turn it around as this upcoming story illustrates.

Hell was about to break out.

My wife, Deborah, and I had taken a day off from work to go hiking to enjoy the changing autumn leaves. We had chosen the middle of the week to avoid the barrage of weekend tourists.

The memory of that day is burned into my mind. We were two hours north of New York City in a national state park that could have been a movie set: the sky was a perfect blue, the air crisp, and the leaves on the trees sparkled with gold, red, and autumn yellow.

Deborah and I were holding hands, laughing, and enjoying everything around us. All of the tension of that week just flowed out and was replaced by a feeling of joy and tranquility.

Then, it got dark. Very dark. And out of fear of getting lost, we quickly hiked back to our car, which by that time was the only car left in the parking lot. And when we got inside, we agreed that a bottle of red wine and a warm meal were next on the agenda.

So I started the car and began to drive out of the lot. And just as suddenly, I stopped. Illuminated by the car lights was a large chain floating over the parking lot exit.

"We're screwed," I thought.

"What do we do now?" I wondered.

"We are stuck in a national state park in the middle of the week. What's the protocol for getting out?" I asked myself.

The look on Deborah's face gave the strong impression she was thinking the same things. "Why don't you look up a number to call?" I suggested. She, on the other hand, thought I should make the call. I am not sure which one of us questioned why we stayed out so late on the hiking trail. Perhaps we both shared that thought. And before we knew it, we got into a fight over what to do next.

Feeling trapped, angry at the situation, and totally frustrated, I decided to drive the car around the posts holding the chain. It was just a small hill I had to transverse, so I gunned the car as my wife screamed out, "Andy, stop! Those rocks will destroy the undercarriage of the car." So I had to stop and was further frustrated because my wife was *absolutely* right.

We sat in the car, staring out at the chain, feeling depressed and defeated. Then, Deborah said three simple words that changed everything.

What were those magic words?

Before answering, let's take a step back and review what happened. We hiked, felt great, were looking forward to going out to dinner, and then saw a chain across the exit. We were locked in. Our thoughts when we first saw the chain were invisible; if you were in the car with us, you wouldn't have known what we were thinking or feeling. The late Chris Argyris, management guru, father of organizational learning, and professor at Harvard Business School,[1] made visible this "invisible process" that formulates our thoughts leading to decisions. He created a mind map illustrating how we "think" called the Ladder of Inference.[2]

Ladder of Inference

Look at the diagram in Figure 1, and you will see that our thought process is like a ladder—each rung has a purpose.

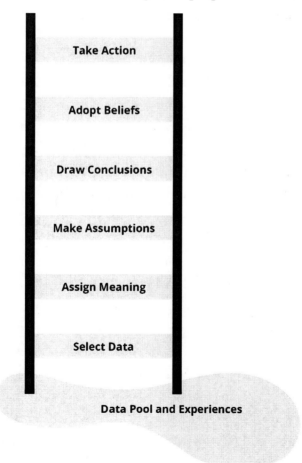

Figure 1. The Ladder of Inference. A mind map created by Chris Argyris.

You begin with collecting data and then sorting through that data to form your assumptions. From there, you draw an inference, making a decision that leads you to an action.

It's a simple and linear process that explains much about our behavior. This is why the Ladder of Inference is so highly respected in the field of learning and development as an instructive metaphor to explain the decision-making process influencing your actions. The "Ladder" serves multiple purposes by helping you become more aware of your thinking, making that thinking visible and a way to probe what others are thinking. Understanding your "true thoughts" leads to smarter decisions.

This does not diminish the value of trusting your "gut." As this book will make clear, however, there are too many decisions to make in the course of just one day, and trusting your instincts alone isn't enough to help you manage these decisions. The Ladder illustrates that the middle rung of every decision is the assumption. In other words, the assumption is one of the key components behind every action. The meaning of this is significant, and I will repeat this point a number of times—that is, making an assumption is as natural as breathing. To judge yourself for making an assumption is nonproductive; you're held back by blaming yourself for an action that is a natural part of the decision-making process.

Instead, recognize that you make assumptions by surfacing them and owning them without guilt. The process of doing this is called making an Assumpt!, and we will explore this process in greater detail in further chapters. What is important to note right now is that once you make an Assumpt!, you have the power to decide if you want to invest in that assumption or challenge it. Challenging your assumptions is what drives creative thinking and problem solving, providing options and alternative ways of attacking a problem or uncovering the answers you seek.

So let's rewind what happened during my autumn excursion. Deborah and I started our hike late on a fall afternoon. As a result, we had to rush back to the trailhead in a relatively short period of time because it was getting dark very quickly. Our relief in getting back to the car transformed into the excitement of heading to a local restaurant for a wonderful meal. As we drove out of the parking lot, the lights of the car illuminated a chain blocking our exit. Being locked out of a national state park generated a high level of stress. All of our good feelings quickly dissipated and were quickly replaced by tension and anxiety, ending in a silly fight. Then, Deborah said three words that changed everything.

"Where's the lock?" she asked.

"Yes, where *is* the lock?" I replied.

So I got out of the car, walked over to the chain, and saw there was no lock. The chain was just hooked to two posts. So I unhooked one of those posts, walked back to the car, and that's when I noticed the sheet of paper under the windshield wipers on the driver's side. I didn't initially see it when I got in the car because it was pitch black outside, and when I had turned on the car, my eyes had followed the illumination of the headlights. The paper read, "If you leave the park after dark, just unhook the chain, and then make sure you rehook the chain on your way out."

I got back in the car, showed Deborah the notice, and we both laughed at the situation. After following these simple instructions, we headed off to what turned out to be a wonderfully romantic dinner.

Jumping the Rung

Let's analyze this situation in terms of the Ladder of Inference and its rungs (Figure 2).

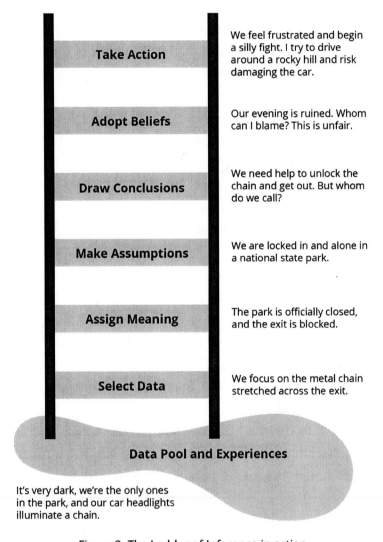

Take Action

We feel frustrated and begin a silly fight. I try to drive around a rocky hill and risk damaging the car.

Adopt Beliefs

Our evening is ruined. Whom can I blame? This is unfair.

Draw Conclusions

We need help to unlock the chain and get out. But whom do we call?

Make Assumptions

We are locked in and alone in a national state park.

Assign Meaning

The park is officially closed, and the exit is blocked.

Select Data

We focus on the metal chain stretched across the exit.

Data Pool and Experiences

It's very dark, we're the only ones in the park, and our car headlights illuminate a chain.

Figure 2. The Ladder of Inference in action

The Ladder of Inference in Action

Data Pool and Experiences

It was dark when Deborah and I got back to the car after the hike. So it's understandable that we didn't see the notice stuck to the window. The darkness amplified the experience of feeling isolated and alone in the park.

Select Data

Then, as we approached the exit, the car lights illuminated the chain.

Assign Meaning

Our immediate thought was that they had closed the park and our exit was blocked.

Make Assumptions

Therefore, we thought we were alone and locked in a state park. It would be hours before we could get out, and our evening was ruined.

Draw Conclusions

We needed to call someone to get out. But what number should we call? Who should make the call? Did our smartphones have enough reception? Why didn't we turn around sooner?

Adopt Beliefs

We were screwed.

Take Action

Rather than verify the data, we invested in our assumption, got into a silly fight, and almost ruined the carriage of the car.

An assumption is something you treat as a fact without any evidence or first verifying that evidence. These assumptions influence our ability to observe and select data objectively from the beginning, so our view of reality gets more distorted as we move up the Ladder, adding meaning and making further assumptions that shape our conclusions, the beliefs we adopt, and the actions we take. As the Ladder of Inference shows, your assumptions are a key driver of your thinking and doing.

For instance, say you send an important text or email to a client with a request to meet. Two days later, you still have no response. If you're like most of us, you'll probably begin to make a number of assumptions related to what you said, how you said it, and how the client feels about you. At this point, nothing is real because you have no feedback from the client. But your assumption doesn't see it that way. Rather than sending a simple follow-up communication, you spend valuable time reworking the email, second-guessing what you might have said, and perhaps taking a negative posture, defending your request to get together.

I admit it's becoming a trend that a lack of response is in some ways a reply. But for people you have relationships with, it is often the case of a delayed reply, lost communication, or a scheduling issue. That's why I suggest that when you don't hear back, don't react as if it's the "chain" blocking your exit. Instead, judge your reaction as an assumption, and take control. Perhaps you could send a simple follow-up such as, "Did you get my request for a meeting?" or "Resending request for meeting. Know how busy you are." This usually works in generating a response, though it may not be the response you're looking for. But at least you'll know the reality and can make smart decisions moving forward.

Chains Confine. So Do Your Assumptions.

Here is a situation in which an assumption keeps you locked in from winning new business. It's a true story, but it's written as if it happened to you.

A former client working at a new company reaches out to you. She has spoken to her boss regarding your firm's past successes, and her boss requested to meet with you. This is a great opportunity as this company is growing quickly and needs help in IT, which is your firm's specialty.

Based on past experiences, you assume this is a "meet-and-greet" kind of occasion as your former client quickly sets up the meeting, reiterating that her boss is really looking forward to getting together. So you bring to the meeting another key person from your company in anticipation of sharing the firm's credentials and answering questions.

Within the first fifteen minutes of the meeting, however, disaster strikes. The boss is asking specific, tactical questions regarding costs and timing. Remember, this is a new firm that is growing rapidly and knows nothing about IT. It turns out their management assumed you would be presenting a complete plan of action, even though they supplied no information.

Unfortunately, you are never given a second chance to come back and present what they were looking for. Within five years, the firm will spend hundreds of millions in new IT. You wince at the lost opportunity every time you see one of its IT platforms in action.

What could have been done differently?

It is so easy to take someone at the face value of what he or she said. In this case, "the boss wants to meet you" seems fairly clear, especially as it was reiterated a number of times by the person setting up the meeting. What was not factored into the equation was the sophistication of the company's leaders. As novices in IT, they did not share the same assumptions regarding the processes that make your firm a success. They assumed your firm could naturally conjure up an IT plan of action without having any input. After all, you and your firm are renowned experts in this field.

It would have been fairly simple to poke holes in your initial assumption that it was a credentials meeting by asking your contact for an agenda instead of bringing your own. This would have raised red flags to what was actually expected from the meeting. The agenda would have quickly disproved the point that you were operating on and changed the course of the meeting and, potentially, the outcome. Again, there is nothing wrong with making an assumption, but it can be costly when that assumption goes unchecked.

Understanding Your Assumptions
to Make Smarter Decisions

1 **Identify an important action you are about to take.** For example, I have a meeting with my new boss who is micromanaging our project. I am going to confront him.

2 **What assumption is this action based on?** Honesty is the best policy, and being vulnerable about the issue will influence my boss's behavior. Especially since I am right.

3 **Try to disprove that assumption without editing yourself. Be honest about the potential outcome you are not seeing.** My boss is not going to change his leadership

style based on my openness, and the conversation may end up causing more tension.

4 **Explore these alternate assumptions to help provide a different perspective and to break any potential chains that may be holding you back.** I will use the meeting to learn more about my new boss and what makes him tick. Perhaps I will not change him, but by winning his trust, he will back off a bit.

Breaking the Chain

Let's go back to the moment that Deborah and I saw the chain. What did we assume?

We assumed we were "locked in." That little assumption changed everything; one minute we were feeling happy and close, and the next, we were tense and on opposite sides of the court.

In other words, the reality hadn't changed. But our assumptions had changed our reality. Just as importantly, the assumption directed our focus to the problem, not on seeking more data or making alternative meanings. As we will explore shortly, people often make assumptions from the get-go that frame their reality. It's quite common to employ your assumptions before verifying the data versus verifying the data to form an assumption.

I spoke with Scott E. Strenger in great length about how we often "skip a rung on the ladder."[3] Strenger is an engineering team leader at a technology company and multiplatform service that helps media companies better engage with customers. Strenger, who is both passionate about his work and highly energetic, focuses on the collection and analysis of customer data.

He shared with me that in his experience, when people begin sourcing through the data, they start looking for the data that will tell them what they already assume. His job is to counter that behavior, encouraging us to "test what you believe, [and] if the data doesn't prove that, then you say, 'Maybe what I believe is wrong.'"[4]

In other words, what happened to my wife and me on that fall day happens everyday in business and in our personal lives. How often do you feel locked out of an opportunity? Or that the solution you are looking for is beyond your reach? Have you ever felt that the project you are working on is overwhelming because it will take forever (so you never begin)? Perhaps you feel an incredible pressure to produce "results" very quickly and are frustrated that the answers aren't coming fast enough.

The key message is to be aware of the power of your assumptions in influencing the data you choose. In future chapters, we will explore why these barriers are often self-inflicted by your assumptions.

Having the ability to identify your assumptions is the first step in the process of discovering potentially better answers. It begins by removing your own prejudice that making assumptions is a bad thing. In reality, assumptions are neither good nor bad. If anything, your assumptions are "friends" that help you process information quickly and, when challenged, open new doors. But, at the same time, assumptions can sometimes be "foes" that lead you, real or not, into a brick wall.

What's important is that you recognize your assumptions without judgment and begin to "own" them. This can be a bit scary at first because facing your assumptions means questioning your beliefs and perhaps doubting them. Just as frightening is knowing there may be another way of doing something, a method you've never tried before. In essence, owning your assumptions comes with understanding that you may have to change the way you are presently doing things. More often than not, it's just as easy to deny these revelations and avoid the anxiety.

But what if owning your assumptions comes with a bigger reward than avoiding them? The sooner you discover this for yourself, the faster you begin to control your assumptions rather than having them control you. Instead of assuming someone is a jerk, you might discover this person proves to be your best business partner. Rather than assuming the budget you inherited will be your undoing, you discover that it's not the budget holding your back but an antiquated process that can be reversed, making you and your team heroes.

The next time you feel trapped, turn those assumptions that are holding you back into ideas that propel you forward. This gives you the competitive advantage as you "drive out of the exit" and look back while others still stare at the "chain."

Let me offer one prescription for doing this. It's just what the doctor ordered.

CHAPTER 4

Turning a "No" into a "Yes"

There are times in business when it feels like the evil empire is working against you. You face certain antiquated processes that prohibit you from moving forward with an idea. You inherit budgets that are unrealistic in executing a plan. You are forced to work with people who continually slow down your efforts and keep getting in the way. You are convinced that the odds are against you. In times like these, consider the biblical story of David and Goliath. When this shepherd boy offered to go into battle against the giant Goliath, he rejected what everyone assumed to be the necessary equipment for battle: a sword and a tunic. Instead, David stepped into the arena with laughable weapons: a stone and a sling. Yet what happened? David slayed Goliath. This chapter is about equipping yourself with a strategy to win by giving yourself permission to put the odds in your favor by simply changing the rules.

Have you ever impatiently waited for an elevator to arrive, pressing the button multiple times to make it come faster? This irrational behavior mirrors how we often deal with conflict. We keep approaching the issue the same way, even though our solutions aren't working. During the 1980's, banks became highly dependent on using direct mail to generate new credit card customers. By the 1990's, the use of direct mail was so overused that mailboxes were being stuffed like turkeys, and the effectiveness of this media began to dwindle. It's a similar issue with email today. But what did the banks do? Instead of trying new methods to increase the odds of success, they increased the expenditure on their direct mail programs, and their return on investments plummeted even further. It was like telling a joke and no one laughs. And, rather than find another joke, you repeat it as if suddenly people will find it funny.

One of my favorite examples of how to turn the odds around and stack them in your favor is in the making of the first James Bond movie, *Dr. No*.

Dr. No and His Aquarium

Ken Adam was at the forefront of film history as the production designer for the original James Bond series. He introduced us to many of Bond's signature gadgets: an Aston Martin with real ejection seats, a forty-foot yacht that could split in two while still moving, and jetpacks that could lift a man a hundred feet into the air.[1] One of Adam's greatest challenges, however, was on the set design of the first James Bond film, *Dr. No*.

For those who don't remember, *Dr. No* was the first Bond movie, released in 1962. It introduced Sean Connery as 007, who upon investigating suspicious activity in Jamaica, ends up disrupting the villainous mission of a diabolical scientist whose name is the title of the film. The existence of Dr. No and his plan takes a while to be revealed as Bond investigates the unexplained disappearance of a British intelligence chief based in Jamaica. While there, he escapes being kidnapped, poisoned by a tarantula, and attacked by a CIA agent whom he ends up befriending. All the clues lead Bond onto a mysterious island inhabited by a fire-breathing dragon.

There he encounters the beautiful Honey Ryder (Ursula Andress) diving for shells. Together they confront the dragon, a flame-throwing tank commanded by Dr. No's private army of solders. Taken prisoner, they finally get to meet their villain who reveals his plot to foil a space launching from Cape Canaveral using atomic power to produce a destructive radio beam.

The meeting takes place in a massive underground headquarters featuring one of the most memorable scenes in the film, an underwater lair with a sunken living room and an adjacent ornate dining room. What dominated the living room and made it truly distinctive was a massive glass wall that showcased the sea.

Building a real aquarium proved prohibitively expensive for a film with a budget of just £20,000 for set design.[2] So Adam came up with an idea: they would put a movie screen behind a glass wall and project film onto the screen. With no money to actually go out and film underwater, they settled for stock footage, and then were aghast to find the fish on film were about the size of goldfish. Adam and his crew tried to magnify the fish, but they looked ridiculous. To add, the glass wall distorted the image further.[3] Creating the set seemed impossible given their limited budget.

You have probably encountered the same sort of problem yourself, even if your job isn't creating elaborate sets for major Hollywood films involving an evil genius.

Many times in business the odds seem against you, no matter what you do. For instance, you have a great product that people love, but you lack the funding to invest in advertising to grow the business to the next level, and your cash flow is running dangerously low. Your client has basically signed off on your project, but you can't close the deal because the client is distracted with other issues, and without a contract, you can't keep your team in place. You find the perfect person to fill a job but lack the salary the candidate desires, and you will lose this person if you don't bring him or her on board soon.

These types of scenarios leave you feeling frustrated. You can almost taste the success of your efforts, but that "one thing" is blocking your way.

I can only imagine that Adam felt that way. In the end, however, the aquarium scene in *Dr. No* happened because Adam and crew members did the unexpected in a very simple way that was brilliant and cost nothing.

To understand the power of this solution (to be revealed), let's first examine the assumptions framing the problem. I underlined those assumptions. Perhaps they sound familiar:

- The production budget to build a live aquarium for Dr. No's living room set <u>isn't enough</u>.

- The <u>only solution</u> is to project existing film footage.

- When we blow up the footage, the fish look distorted. <u>We're screwed!</u>

The belief that the "footage isn't going to work" is based on the set designer's and film director's experience; using distorted film will raise creative aesthetic issues and more importantly run the risk of the viewer feeling it's out of place.

But what if you tossed out the assumptions underlined above? What if you forced yourself to look at the problem in a completely different light? What if the solution had nothing to do with dollars spent on the set?

Strategy: Write Your Own Script

In the case of *Dr. No*, an ingenious yet simple solution was generated that required neither money nor additional time. What was the secret?

The team simply altered the wording of the movie script! This brilliant yet simple idea allowed the viewer to accept that the film footage was actually distorted (because it was) without disrupting the flow of the action. Below in boldface is the copy that was changed, allowing the viewer to accept the low-quality footage as part of the movie reality.

> Dr. No: You were admiring my aquarium.
>
> Bond: Yes. It's quite impressive.
>
> Dr. No: A unique feat of engineering if I say so. I designed it myself. The glass is convex. 10 inches thick, **which accounts for the magnifying effect.**
>
> **Bond: Minnows pretending they are whales. Just like you on this island, Dr. No.**
>
> **Dr. No: It depends Mr. Bond, on which side of the glass you are.**[4]

This conversation between Dr. No and James Bond lasts no more than a minute, but it accounted for the distortion effect and allowed for one of the most memorable scenes in the Bond canon to remain intact. Director Terence Young and script assistant Johanna Harwood are often credited with rewriting this scene on the fly. Ken Adam said he was also involved.

In this case, the assumption that "it's impossible" to use distorted film footage was challenged by changing the script, an important strategy that can be used in managing your own assumptions once you identify them. *Writing your own script* is a very valuable tool in this process and especially handy when faced with "it-can't-be-done" scenarios. Writing your own script is about giving yourself permission to explore changing the rules you impose on yourself or the ways of doing things within your organization and among your team.

Let's take a look at another example that plays out in the world of cyberespionage but has applications in your business and life. We'll begin with another piece of fiction and moviemaking.

Star Trek: **Writing a Script for Cheating**

Fans of the science-fiction TV show *Star Trek* are familiar with the term *Kobayashi Maru*, which is another term for a no-win situation. Think of something like having to jump out of a burning plane with no parachute. Or having to produce a room-sized aquarium without having the proper budget to do so.

In the movie *Star Trek II: The Wrath of Khan* (1982), Captain James T. Kirk, played by William Shatner, reveals his character when he faces a Kobayashi Maru scenario in the form of a computer flight simulation. It occurs when he is a young cadet and ordered to save a stranded spaceship disabled in enemy territory. But that's where the no-win scenario unfolds: it's actually a trap. So saving the ship means the destruction of his spacecraft, but choosing not to mount the rescue mission will result in the destruction of the stranded spaceship.

Captain Kirk, however, beats the program and ensures he will win by hacking into the system and rewriting the flight program before he faces the simulation.[5] In a much later release, *Star Trek* (2009), Kirk, played by Chris Pine, is initially accused of "cheating" but is later awarded a special citation by the Starfleet academy for "thinking differently" about confronting the overall challenge.[6]

It's easy to assume that a fictitious concept has little relevance for today's real business and life issues. Yet Gregory Conti, an associate professor in the United States Military Academy's Department of Electrical Engineering and Computer Science, and James Caroland, an adjunct associate professor in the University of Maryland University College's Cybersecurity program, would argue differently.

The pair performed a fascinating experiment designed to help students of cybersecurity think differently by giving them a seemingly "impossible" task.[7] Students needed to solve a problem that required memorization but whose answer could not be memorized: the first one hundred digits of pi. The only solution was to cheat, and their grade was dependent on their level of creativity in finding a way to do so. Put another way, students faced their own Kobayashi Maru: they had to cheat to pass the test.

But the teachers had another catch: if students got caught cheating, they would fail.

Students' solutions were both amusing and impressive. One student used his Mandarin Chinese skills to hide the answers. Another put the answer on a soda can, which could be turned away from the proctor as he walked by. The winning student used a false book cover in which the answer was coded on the back cover.

The premise behind this exercise was that "cheating will challenge students' assumptions about security and the trust models they envision."[8] According to the professors of the course, it is through "learning the thought processes of our adversaries that we can hope to unleash the creative thinking needed to build the best secure systems, become effective at red teaming and penetration testing, defend against attacks, and conduct ethical hacking activities."[9]

The purpose of this research was to help these students become more responsible in this field. According to the professors, "By anticipating such actions and reactions, ethical actors are far better prepared to build secure systems and perform both defensive and offensive activities successfully."[10]

In short, thinking like the enemy helps you defeat the enemy. Thinking like your competition helps you win against them. Thinking like your boss helps you understand him or her. Thinking like your peers helps you ensure alignment with them. We will explore the very important skill of seeing the world through the other person's eyes in an upcoming chapter.

In the case of cyberespionage, thinking like the adversary doesn't mean you have to act like one. But not thinking like the adversary is cheating yourself from being one step ahead of the enemy. And that is a terrible crime.

I invite you to experiment with the strategy of *writing your own script* by trying the upcoming exercise. You might be surprised at how easy it is to write your own happy ending, even when faced with an impossible choice.

After that, let's move on to the next chapter (Chapter 5) to help you better understand where your assumptions come from, how to spot them, and what drives them.

What Script Are You Reading From?

"You define your own life. Don't let other people write your script." —Oprah Winfrey[11]

As mentioned before, in life we don't face many real Kobayashi Marus. But we often face what we perceive to be Kobayashi Marus. Take the following scenarios:

- You have sixteen days to execute a new marketing plan that was estimated to take ninety days to complete.

- You have a budget of $5 million to revamp your IT infrastructure, which is one-fifth of the budget you proposed.

- Your top manager just resigned on the day you are beginning a new business-consulting project, and that manager was the one the client was expecting to show up.

As impossible as these situations appear, the history of business has demonstrated that solutions are at hand. You just have to give yourself permission to create them.

1 **Identify a goal you are trying to achieve.** Does it relate to any of the scenarios above? Are you facing an impossible timing, budget, or management issue?

2 **Now, write a script based on how things are going.** For example, you've just found out your competition is launching its marketing campaign using media you can't afford. Or the IT platform you recommend and were moving forward with is no longer an option as your budget got cut. Perhaps the manager who just left hasn't trained a replacement, and you know little about this specific department.

3 **Now, give yourself permission to rewrite the script so that the story ends the way you want it to.** What elements do you need to change? How can you change the objectives, alter the specifications, or rearrange the players? For example, a company lacked the marketing staff and advertising budget to compete with its competitors who were five times its size. Therefore, in launching its service, the company wrote its own script by playing to its strength: its smaller size allowed for a better class of customer service than its giant competitors (think David and Goliath). The story had a happy ending as the business turned its customers into marketing advocates, which proved more powerful than spending money in traditional media. In other words, the business wrote its own script for marketing and advertising rather than following the traditional and expected path others in its industry were using.

There will always be reasons why something can't be accomplished—namely, lack of time, money, or resources. However, by giving yourself permission to change the rules, you create a new playing field that may change the odds and allow you to turn a "No, that's impossible to do" into a "Yes, here is how it can be done."

CHAPTER 5

How to Spot Your Assumptions
Before It's Too Late

You're the captain of a ship on a voyage through the Arctic Ocean and discover you are heading directly toward an iceberg. Immediately, you slow down and begin to plot a new course because you know the potential danger (90 percent of that iceberg lies under the sea). As discussed, assumptions are subconscious, and you are not aware you are making them until the damage is already done. So you need to find cues that signal an assumption is being made. Certain words and phrases, like the tip of the iceberg, hint at what could lie beneath the surface. This chapter will help you use these cues and enhance your radar to spot your assumptions.

Wouldn't it be nice if you could be aware of all your assumptions before you acted upon them? You'd minimize the number of people you judged unfairly. You could stop yourself from making that costly decision that hurt your business or job. Perhaps you could have avoided the unnecessary tension generated by misunderstanding what someone just said to you.

But the luxury of instantly spotting your assumptions would also include the curse of overanalyzing everything: driving a car would become impossible because of the time it would take to review making a right turn before making it, and answering a simple question would take half an hour because you would explore every facet and angle to make sure you got it right.

As mentioned before, addressing every assumption you make isn't practical. Still, this creates a dilemma. If assumptions by nature are taken for granted and subconscious, then they are "invisible." So how do you make them visible? And how do you know which to make "visible" and then challenge?

Let's tackle the easier question first: How do I spot, or "surface," my assumptions? The second question regarding which assumptions to invest in challenging requires a different set of guidelines and will be discussed in Parts 2 and 3.

Making the Invisible Visible

Having a tool set to identify your assumptions is crucial. Your assumption happens in a nanosecond, and you are already acting on it before you can even reflect on it. For example, imagine someone walking into the room right now. Would you be able to delay any judgments, viewing this person in complete objectivity until you gather all the facts, ask questions, and see how others react to him or her?

I can't. Instead, I recognize I am making a number of assumptions that formulate my opinion. My Assumpt! (reminder: this word acknowledges that I am making an assumption) is that I am not the only one who instinctually reads into a person's personality when shaking hands for the first time. After all, this form of communication dates back to Roman times when it was conjectured that the handshake served to establish hidden weaponry. Over time, the handshake has taken on many meanings, from binding contracts to establishing trust. In Western business, a firm grip signals a person's strength and level of confidence. But this is just an assumption as most of the world's successful businesspeople employ a less firm, weaker grip.

My business takes me across the globe, and I have become distinctly aware of how easy it is to start making assumptions during the process of reaching out and grabbing someone's hand. It has taught me how quickly our assumptions come into play when dealing with cultural differences. This awareness allows me to keep an open mind rather than immediately invest in dangerous assumptions that influence my judgments.

Often, I am not sure of the depth of those assumptions. The key is that I don't judge myself for making them. This simple act allows the assumptions to percolate up from my subconscious and clearly formulate. It's as if you "freeze" time for a second to create breathing space before investing too heavily in something you are thinking that may not be true. Doing this helps you seek confirmations of those assumptions in a more objective way—you ask questions about the person, listen to the person, and see how others react to the person. This allows you to generate a purer picture of that person, situation, or conversation and reroute your surfaced assumptions to formulate a different and perhaps truer sense of the reality facing you.

A radio talk-show host shared a story about his first job as a car salesman.[1] One day, a customer walked in wearing blue jeans and looking like he had just come off the field after a day of plowing. All the other salespeople assumed that this "farmer" would only want the cheapest car. The radio host didn't share their assumptions. What he saw was a customer, and he engaged him in conversation, asking questions and exploring his needs. The interaction ended with the young salesman closing the deal and the customer buying one of the most expensive cars on the lot.

Yes, often your initial assumptions are correct, even if you are not aware you are making them. But it's the ones you are not even considering, the ones three layers down in your subconscious, that can mess you up. For example, an assistant I hired commented on my company's website, which cost significant time and money to produce. She thought it was "lacking energy." I dismissed this observation, assuming she lacked experience in my business and feeling confident that the website had been developed by talented people. A year later, it dawned on me that her lack of experience had nothing to do with her observation that proved to be correct. As a result, I lost valuable time in revamping the website because of a deeply embedded assumption.

So how do we surface these assumptions so that we can address them at the moment we make them rather than after the fact or when it is too late?

Your Verbal Cues

An effective way to identify assumptions around sizing up other people is by first sizing up yourself, listening to what you are thinking or saying.

Over time, I have observed a number of phrases that represent a dangerous assumption driving a conversation or an action. And I have shared these verbal cues with participants in my keynotes and executive seminars. You might say them out loud or simply think them, but either way, these words serve as valuable tools to helping you spot a variety of different assumptions in your day-to-day activities.

Let's start with one verbal cue we have all said more than we might like to admit: "I can't."

"I can't get this done in time." "I can't figure this out." "I can't get anyone to return my texts." "I can't do this on my own." "I can't learn this new system." "I can't get my customer to say yes." "I can't draw a straight line."

I didn't realize how often I said, "I can't" until I began to see it as an assumption versus a perceived momentary reality.

For example, I was looking to create a new website on a limited budget. This site required particular skills that were beyond my costs. Soon, I found myself telling a few associates that "I can't find the right resource" or "I can't get this done on the budget I have." I felt stuck. I am a firm believer that the more you invest in the negative, the more it strengthens the perceived reality. So if you keep saying you're "stuck," the more real the situation feels, and the harder it becomes to be "unstuck." The more you say, "I can't," the more you "can't" do what you want to do.

You can break this habit, however, by seeing this verbal statement as a cue that you are making an assumption. "I can't" might really mean that you don't want to do something, are afraid of doing it differently, or are having trouble finding the right resources to help you complete the job. Within a fraction of a second of recognizing "I can't" as an assumption, an array of new doors open, leading to a pathway of ideas for finding the solution you are looking for.

"I can't" is also a very dangerous assumption because it instantly makes you powerless, robbing you of your real potential. True, I would love to be a professional punter in American football, but I can't because I am over thirty, haven't kicked a football in a few years, and lack the training. Still, more often than not, when I mutter these two words, it's related to completely different issues that are under my control but don't feel that way. I have found that "I can't" most often means "I don't know how," "I don't want to wait," or "I don't want to spend the time working on this."

Here is another common phrase that can wreak havoc on your business as the pace of technology continues to quicken.

If you find yourself saying with complete confidence, "I know who my competition is," realize you are making an assumption. Reflect on why you believe this. Consider what you would find if you looked in unexpected places.

Those who own their own businesses can reflect on how often they felt on top of their game by knowing exactly who their competition was. They can also reflect on how, all of a sudden, they were losing business to a company they had never even heard of.

Think of BlackBerry, the once high-tech gadget company that at the turn of the millennium created a unique mobile device containing a distinctive and robust business email application delivered on a proprietary cell phone with keyboard. It's easy to forget there was once a time when emails had to be downloaded manually in order to be read. BlackBerry's application, however, allowed emails to be "pushed," or automatically received. Business embraced this technology, and in 2009, BlackBerry was on track to be one of the fastest-growing companies in North America. Its application was so popular for how quickly email could be delivered and how easily its keyboard could be used that it bred the term *CrackBerry* to describe people's addiction to constantly reading and responding to their emails.

BlackBerry assumed its competition would come from other companies offering similar "enterprise" services to businesses. But this assumption proved deadly as the company ignored the high-speed technology advances in the consumer world driven by Apple and Google.

BlackBerry's focus on its unique keyboard, for example, kept it from evolving phone technology at a time when the consumer industry was moving to the touch screens offered by smartphones. As it turned out, business users favored this consumer technology as well.

In early 2010, BlackBerry's US market share was over 40 percent. Two-and-a-half years later, it was below 10 percent.[2] It's dangerous to assume that you truly "know your competition."

This may be one reason companies like Uber, PayPal, and Tesla fight so hard to establish unique services and products in order to become the monopoly for that product or service. They understand how easy it is for unseen competition to grow from nothing into owning the marketplace in what appears to be "overnight." After all, that's exactly what they did.

As mentioned, I've been collecting and studying the different types of assumptions individuals and groups make about themselves, others, and their circumstances. The result is a database of verbal cues that helps to more quickly identify that an assumption is being made.

Meet Your DAD

Since the saying goes that "assumptions are the mother of all screw-ups," I decided to call this database of assumptions *DAD*, for Dangerous Assumptions Database. Listening to business owners, CEOs, and senior leaders and their teams over the past few years has provided an intensive list of dangerous assumptions that haunt organizations. Drawing upon this list, I have also invited a diverse number of professionals to contribute their own dangerous assumptions.

A partial list is included in the back of this book (Appendix A), but you can start your own list right now by noting, at the end of each day, the assumptions you've made that acted as barriers to change or that had unpleasant consequences. Learn from them, and let them become your own DAD. Perhaps you will even share them with us by sending an email to DAD@andycohen.com.

The Dangerous Assumptions Database functions by helping you identify assumptions through hearing yourself or others say them. My Assumpt! is that if you review them a few times, it will help sensitize you to the next time a particular dangerous assumption is thought or discussed. Remember that these symptoms and clues can be applied not only to you but also to those you are interacting with. The more you can recognize the symptoms and clues of others, the more effective you will be in responding to what they are assuming rather than just saying.

For example, Figure 3 shows five dangerous assumptions from DAD that a packaged-goods company encouraged me to share with its sales force:

5 Dangerous Assumptions

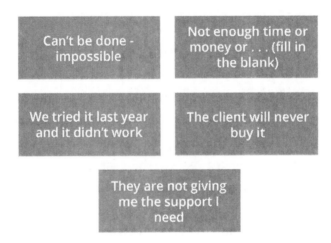

Figure 3. Five dangerous assumptions from DAD

You will notice these are common and frequent forms of assumptions everyone makes. They can be heard when a cost-cutting strategy goes into effect, sales quotas are increased, and divisions are merged. When people say, "We don't have enough money (or time, resources, fill in the blank)," it's often driven by an assumption. The lack of money is a reality to deal with but is often not the major roadblock to accomplishing the task.

For example, the time it takes to make a decision is often a function of the time you have to make that decision. Suppose you feel you don't have enough time to make a decision, so you say to someone, "I need more time," and the person responds with, "You have an hour." Do you think you can formulate a decision within that time frame? My Assumpt! is that you can.

Take a look at the assumptions from DAD, listed on the next page, and choose the ones that resonate the most with you. Then, test them out. Every time you hear yourself or someone else say these assumptions, don't respond immediately. Instead, let the assumptions associated with these words and phrases percolate and surface. Now, you are ready to explore them using a technique we will discuss in Chapter 8: Challenging Your Assumpts!

One of my favorite dangerous assumptions is that "the client will never buy it." Many times, I have watched people dismiss their own ideas before they even present them. They will start by saying, "This idea is too far out there, and you won't like it. But let me share it with you anyway." More often than not, this is the idea that has the greatest potential and is the most compelling.

Why do people assume that "the client will never buy it"? For many reasons. Sometimes, it's driven by power. These individuals will say with the utmost confidence that their client won't buy it to reinforce how well they know the client and how important they are to that relationship. It has nothing to do with the quality of the thinking.

But when the client sees the idea, it's love at first sight.

Other times, an idea seems too risky to invest in, and "the client will never buy it" reflects a fear to support something that has a chance of failing. When *Seinfeld*, the TV comedy, was piloted, it scored poorly when shown in front of a focus group of viewers. Imagine if the person in charge of programming assumed that "the client (my viewers) will never buy it" because of the research. I am not privy to why the network didn't follow that assumption, but I am glad they stood their ground as *Seinfeld* turned into one of the longest-running comedies in TV history.

Have fun familiarizing yourself with the following examples, taken from the Dangerous Assumptions Database in Appendix A. After you review these dangerous assumptions, let's move on and take a look at what drives them. After all, knowing where they come from helps you figure out where to take them.

Competition

We are the smartest of all our competitors.

We're unique. No one is like us.

I know who my competition is.

Consumer Behavior and Demand

Our system is easy to use.

Consumers need "us."

The consumer is just like me.

Marketing and Sales

We tried it last year, and it didn't work.

The client will never buy it.

I have a clear understanding of who the decision-maker is.

They are idiots if they don't get the concept.

Leadership and Management

I seem to be the only one worrying about the issues.

If I don't make a decision, then it won't be my fault.

When I speak, my team listens.

My team and my clients make decisions rationally.

I can't admit I don't know or have the answer.

Failure

If I fail, I will lose my job.

There's no difference between a small or large failure. All failures
are the same.

How can I make a decision if I don't have all the facts?
Let someone else make the decision and be wrong.

Customer Experience

This product is a no-brainer.
The consumer won't complain as long as it's free.
Niche is the key.

Public Relations

Getting "ink" (coverage) is the primary goal of public relations.
> If I get written up in *The New York Times* or another well-known publication, we'll have it made.

Any type of coverage is more important than staying consistent.
We can generate sales with just public relations.

IT and Technology

Customers aren't using that technology, so we don't have to care about it.
If they can't understand the directions, then they shouldn't be using the technology.
This is the way I use the product, so customers will or should also.

Start-Ups

This will remain true for twenty years.
Because it's in my plan, I have control over it.
Everyone on the team is aligned in our vision and strategy.

Compliance

I am not the problem.
This is the way they said to do it.
There's no time to be fully engaged.
I follow the rules. It's the other person who doesn't.

Pricing

It costs (this much) to make it. Period.

Customers all understand that a reasonable profit is important.

People will only value something if they pay for it (versus getting it for free).

CHAPTER 6

Where Do Your Assumptions
Come From?

A friend told me this very common yet poignant story, which illustrates well the key message of this chapter:

> A newlywed wanted to surprise her husband for dinner by making a brisket. She set about preparing it, cutting the ends off as she had learned from her mother. When her husband saw this, he asked why had she cut the ends off?
>
> She said, "That's how my mom always made it." Then, out of curiosity, she promptly called her mom.
>
> "Mom, how come you always cut the ends off of the brisket before you cook it"?
>
> "Well, I don't really know—that is just the way that Nana always made the brisket."
>
> They hung up, and her mom promptly called Nana, her mother.
>
> "Mom, how come you always cut the ends off of the brisket"?
>
> "Because the pan was too small."

It's easier to recognize your assumptions when you understand what drives them. This chapter examines four key factors that influence and formulate your beliefs (Figure 4). Knowing these four key factors will help you become more sensitive to the act of making an assumption.

Assumption Generators

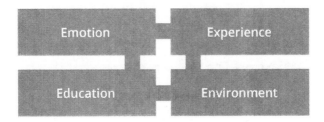

Figure 4. What drives your assumptions? The four key categories.

It is important to note that your assumptions are influenced by more than one category at the same time. For example, your environment influences your assumptions at the same time your experience does. Deborah and I saw the chain at night. We may have had a totally different experience if it was during the day. Or your education and present emotional state combine to create certain underlying assumptions.

After being misdiagnosed for a hand injury by a number of prominent physicians, Dr. Jerome Groopman, chair at Harvard Medical School, decided to write a book, *How Doctors Think*. He recognizes that time and other pressures make it hard to be a physician. But those mistakes often relate to the doctor's thinking rather than technical errors, such as mislabeling a blood test. Under these emotionally stressful situations, a doctor begins to make a diagnosis of a patient's problem within eighteen seconds of seeing him or her. "We make what's called an anchoring mistake—we fix on that snap judgment," said Groopman.[1]

In other words, there may be four separate categories, but more often than not, multiple contributors effect the formulation of your assumptions.

Emotion

Consider how you feel at the end of a frustrating workday during which you ran out of time and nothing seemed to go right. In that state, things often look bleak, and you formulate a number of assumptions that make going to work the next day a bit depressing.

Let's imagine that you have a 10:00 a.m. meeting the next day to present a new pricing strategy. But by the end of today, you still haven't settled on what you will recommend. All the numbers are blending together, and you are losing sight of the big picture. When you think of tomorrow, all you see is a disaster and no resolution in sight.

But you force yourself to get to the gym, go for a bike ride, or play tennis that evening. Or perhaps you play a game, read a book, or eat a fabulous meal. After getting some exercise or separating yourself from your work, you start feeling better, and the pricing strategy all of a sudden falls into place. Your assumptions shifted with your emotional state, and now you can't wait until tomorrow to make the presentation.

How you perceive people is also influenced by how you feel at the moment. In one study, people were asked to evaluate a stranger's personality based on a written description. Those who read the description while holding a steaming cup of coffee saw that stranger's personality as "warmer." Those holding a cold glass of soda in their hand rated that exact same written profile as "colder."[2]

Have you ever been in the supermarket shopping for something like an aspirin? On the shelf is a popular brand. Right next to it is the drugstore's generic version that is significantly less expensive. Do you suddenly debate which to buy even though one costs less and you know that all aspirins are the same? At this point, you are not necessarily thinking logically but emotionally, and a number of assumptions are kicking in. Sure, many brands are distinctive and worthy of the cost differential compared to their competitors. But the purpose of branding is to generate a number of assumptions tied to the emotional appeal of that brand—that you will feel more successful, safer, more comfortable, happier, etc.

Experience

In the beginning of this book, I shared that when my wife and I saw a chain, all of our experience taught us that we were locked out and that by following that assumption blindly, we had actually locked ourselves out.

In business, a company's deep level of experience can dangerously limit its thinking. In 1996, Motorola manufactured and introduced the first clamshell/flip cell phone called the Motorola StarTAC. It was an instant success, and Motorola continued that success into the mid-2000s when introducing the RAZR, one of the thinnest cell phones.

Since post-World War II, Motorola has been an innovative company in radio, satellite, TV, and telecommunications. In 1969, Neil Armstrong's infamous words "one small step for a man, one giant leap for mankind" were transmitted from the Moon via a Motorola transceiver.

The successful experience with StarTAC and then the RAZR drove Motorola's assumption that the world needed a better cell phone, so it kept developing innovative versions. At one point, it had made so many different versions that telecommunications companies like Verizon were complaining of being confused by too many choices and would prefer if Motorola recommended just one or two that they should carry for their customers.

In essence, the company's experience limited its thinking, and it kept creating the best cell phone at a time there was a significant market shift in the growth of smartphones. By the time Motorola realized this, it had locked itself into being the best at something the consumer no longer wanted.

When Sanjay Jha became Motorola's co-CEO in 2008, Motorola's share of the phone market was 7 percent down from 60 percent in 1994, two years before the StarTAC was launched.[3] Almost immediately, Jha forced the company to move out of its comfort level generated by its past experiences and offered to listen to any new ideas feeding growth. An employee suggested Motorola explore a new operating system by Google called Android. A year later, Motorola introduced the first Droid phone, which became a serious challenger to the iPhone and is now one of the two major smartphone operating systems.

Ron Wayne, a middle-aged manager at Atari, had tried, unsuccessfully, to start a slot machine company (it later went bankrupt). Later, he became one of the original partners in Apple, but when it came time to invest more money, he asked to be bought out for initially $800 and eventually another $1,500.[4] His early experience in losing money on a start-up made him assume this was a similar situation and thus the right decision. His initial investment in Apple would be worth more than $2.6 billion today.[5] Wayne is obviously remorseful but stands by his actions: "I made the best decision for me at the time. Both of them were real whirlwinds, and I knew my stomach and it wasn't ready for such a ride."[6]

Perhaps at times when you believe all your experience has made you wiser, consider that this assumption may actually limit your thinking.

Education

Education is a wonderful thing. We need to spend more time

grooming and rewarding teachers, supplying our children with computers to access the web, and spending money on the educational infrastructure. But we must remember that what we are taught can be fallible.

To illustrate, consider Dr. Peter Densen's 2011 paper titled "Challenges and Opportunities Facing Medical Education," which addresses the rapid changes in technology and information. In his paper, Densen discussed the speed in which new medical knowledge was, is, and will be introduced from 1950 to his estimate in 2020. He concluded, "What was learned in the first three years of medical school will be just 6 percent of what is known at the end of the decade from 2010 to 2020. Knowledge is expanding faster than our ability to assimilate and apply it effectively; and this is as true in education and patient care as it is in research."[7]

And once information is entered into the education curriculum, it is hard to remove, even when the information is false. For example, a majority of baby boomers were schooled that Christopher Columbus proved the world was round, not flat as most of Europe believed, and that it took supreme courage to challenge that belief. Trouble is, that's not true. The story about proving the world was flat was created by a highly talented author, Washington Irving, who was frustrated that he was valued for his fables but not his serious writings—so he decided to write a book about Spain, a country he passionately loved. Knowing the value of drama to capture a reader's interest, he injected the "world is flat" story. In 1828, his romanticized biography, *A History of the Life and Voyages of Christopher Columbus*, was published.[8] The reality that a majority of Europeans had known the world was round for hundreds of years didn't matter. It took over 160 years for this "fabled fact" to be removed from American schoolbooks.

When I shared this story with my NYU marketing class, one of the students suddenly looked pained as he raised his hand to comment.

"My teacher growing up taught me that Columbus proved the world was round. Now you, as a professor, are telling me that is not true. I don't know whom to believe," he concluded.

He couldn't have stated the issue more succinctly. It's painful to discover that something from our past education is wrong, no longer useful, or irrelevant. But in today's world of "disruption" in technology, business, and economy, it's highly useful to see education as one dimension of your learning curve—an assumption but not necessarily the determiner of truth.

Every company educates its employees on its culture. Yet a company culture is really a set of assumptions that everyone conforms to. Have you ever experienced the painful transition of moving to another company and discovering that what you learned in your previous job does not align with the new position? Banks and pharmaceutical companies often hire people from consulting firms like McKinsey & Company because they have been educated and trained to think in a particular way that has immeasurable value. At the same time, these consultants often discover, to their frustration, that their new employers are not utilizing the strengths they were hired for because company culture doesn't support them; their assumptions aren't in alignment.

Value what you know. But also know that knowledge drives your assumptions and at times in the wrong direction.

Environment

Most people assume the most important part of any keynote is the content. But the greatest content can be washed away if presented in the wrong space. Configuration is as important as content.

I learned this from a course conducted by Interaction Associates, one of the world's leading firms in teaching facilitation. The workshop was titled "Essential Facilitation," and the workshop leader emphasized to all that the physical setup of a meeting contributes to 50 percent of its success.[9]

This is why I look at the stage, the size of the room, how people are sitting, and the type of lighting on me and above them before giving a seminar or keynote. More often than not, adjustments need to be made (e.g., the room is too dark, so we add more lights, or there are too many seats at a table, so we take some away).

A joint study among several worldwide academics postulated that people actually think more creatively when they sit outside a box versus sitting in the box itself. In the study, titled "Embodied Metaphors and Creative 'Acts,'" they "suggest a connection between concrete bodily experiences and creative cognition."[10]

These examples suggest that your environment influences your perception of the world around you and the productivity of your thinking. This is one reason I use a hydraulic desk that raises and lowers the top of my worktable. I tend to stand up and work at the computer, but after a long day, when I assume that my mind is going blank, I lower the desk to a sitting position and can begin working again. Often, I will change the color of my pen to help me think differently. When I give a keynote, I ask that everything be off the stage (if possible) as it makes me feel more "open" and helps "declutter" my message to my audience.

Now that you know how to recognize assumptions and what drives them, let's move to Part 2 and explore the Assumpt! strategy that turns your dangerous assumptions into opportunities.

PART 2

Turning Your Assumptions into Opportunities

Part 1 of this book focused on helping you acknowledge that you make daily assumptions in all aspects of business and life, that there is nothing wrong with making them, and that if assumptions are not recognized, they can be quite dangerous.

Part 1 also provided you ways to surface and identify these subconscious thoughts through verbal cues and appreciation for what drives them.

Part 2 will now explore a process and provide tools for how to turn your assumptions into opportunities. It all begins with the Assumpt!

CHAPTER 7

The Assumpt!

The difference between the words "assumption" and "Assumpt!" is symbolic. Your assumption turns into your Assumpt! the moment you become aware that you are taking something for granted or treating a belief as fact or truth. Once you gain that awareness, you can begin to manage your Assumpt!, which will be explained shortly. Let's first explore how to use the Assumpt! strategically.

The Assumpt! is a strategy for empowering yourself with the ability to make smarter decisions and generate better outcomes, thus helping you overcome barriers standing in the way of your success. This is achieved by helping you think and act differently in three main ways:

- acknowledging that it's normal to make assumptions

- learning to recognize your assumptions before you act

- having a process and the tools to manage your assumptions when you choose to do so

You can't spell-check the term *Assumpt!* I created the term for the practical reason that it sticks with you. It is not uncommon that within twenty minutes after a lecture or seminar, a person or group will be heard saying, "That's an Assumpt!"

The term's stickiness is its strength, as we all need a reminder that the daily things we take for granted, things that we take at face value and just accept "as is," are assumptions that directly affect our outcomes. Surfacing our assumptions turns them into Assumpts!

Having this awareness means that if you change your assumptions into Assumpts!, you can change your outcomes. Consider how the production and film crew on the set of *Dr. No* changed their assumptions and found a way to circumvent the cost of building a set they couldn't afford.

The key thought here is that if you don't manage your assumption, your assumption will automatically manage you. If you always blindly follow your assumptions, you will have less control over the results of your actions. Reflect on the catastrophe of the Mars Orbiter when engineers gave up control by assuming each was using the same measuring system.

Here is a brief list of things you can control better when you turn your assumptions into Assumpts!

- how people react to what you say
- your ability to solve a difficult problem
- how well you manage an employee
- exceeding monthly sales projections
- zeroing in on your customers' needs
- successfully hiring a new employee
- getting someone to agree with your idea
- doubling your monthly profit

Why the "!" at the End of Assumpt!?

Having the ability to control outcomes and generate new opportunities is quite satisfying and is the reason the "!" appears at the end of the word *Assumpt!* This form of punctuation reflects the emotional satisfaction and surprise one feels when solving a problem or avoiding one, whether ordinary or insurmountable. The relief you feel when stopping yourself from getting into a fight. The pride you get when doubling your product sales by shifting media expenditures in an unexpected way. The intrinsic satisfaction you get in a job offer from a company that shares your values, a company you had never even considered working for.

John Danner is a management consultant, entrepreneur, and professor at the University of California, Berkeley, and Princeton University. He is also coauthor of *The Other "F" Word: How Smart Leaders, Teams, and Entrepreneurs Put Failure to Work*, a definitive exploration of how failure affects leaders, teams, and entrepreneurs. One day when discussing the role of the "!" with Danner, he had an epiphany regarding how punctuation underscores the entire Assumpt! concept.[1] Springboarding off his insights brought me to an explanation that helps further clarify the function of the Assumpt! It also sets up the background for how to challenge your Assumpts! It begins with the "."

The period.

In most Western languages, you add a period, or *full stop* (the British term), at the end of a sentence without even thinking. It's a standard operating procedure for almost all languages to indicate a complete thought. It also reflects a definitive and closed statement.

The assumption has much in common with the period. It's mostly made without thinking. It's a standard operating procedure in any decision. It's quite definitive as it leads you in only one direction when it goes unchecked. And it stops conversation in its tracks.

For example, "I will see you at eight on the tennis court" seems clear and contained. That is, until you show up at eight in the morning and your partner isn't there because he assumed eight at night (I should know because this happened to me).

Here are other examples. When a chief marketing officer of a company says, "We have no competition," the officer is making a very clear statement that lacks an invitation to disagree. When one of your employees in charge of production tells you that the new project on hand "is a no-brainer," the employee is indicating there is no need for further discussion, as the project will take care of itself. If a team leader thinks, "They get what I am saying," then there is no need to repeat the message as it's assumed everyone listened with full comprehension. These statements often go unchallenged because as the "." reflects, they are treated as definitive like the end of a line (excuse the double entendre). For example, have you ever heard someone say, "That's it, and no more. Period."?

The functional similarity between this form of punctuation and thought process is why I assigned the "." to symbolize the assumption.

This metaphoric period, or full stop, represents your assumption that when not acknowledged, or followed blindly, leads your thinking in one direction, like a lemming who behaves as if there is just one way to go: over the edge of the cliff.

Different Figures. Same Purpose.

A *sentence* by definition is a set of words that makes a complete thought.

When a one-dimensional pinpoint is used at the end of a sentence, it indicates that the thought is definitive. The definitive nature of this punctuation is especially made clear when someone says, "The earth is flat, period" or "This is the strategy to go with, period."

Different languages and different cultures have different punctuations to signal the end of a sentence. The British and Americans use the "." Hindi uses a vertical line |. *Amharic*, the official language of Ethiopia, uses four dots ∷ that look like two side-by-side colons. Simplified Chinese uses a small circle called 句号 (pronounced jùhào, meaning *sentence mark*). For simplicity, I will use the term *period* as indicated by a small speck: ".".

Now, let's experiment and turn the "period" into something completely different by adding what looks like an upside-down hook on top of it: "?"

Now, we have a question.

Grammatically, the "?" serves many purposes: it creates doubt, invites investigation, promotes conversation, and publicly states that something is unknown.

Thus, "There is no competition" converts to "Is there competition?" Now, the point under discussion is reframed. Instead of everything moving ahead, things stop as the "question mark" automatically creates a pause, a vacuum in space that needs to be filled. Perhaps there is competition that we haven't measured or don't see. Maybe our definition of *competition* is too narrow. Could it be that technology is allowing other companies to do more things than we do?

When listening to spoken English and French, you can often hear the question in the speakers' intonations, whether or not the sentence itself is in the form of a question. The sentence rises at the end, inviting exploration. In simplified Chinese, the characters representing the question mark, 问号 (pronounced wènhào), also mean "unknown factor" and "unsolved problem." The first character combines the radical for door with the radical for mouth. It is the sign of an opening. This is significant as the function of a "question" is to go from closing a door to opening one.

This pause created by the "?" is quite powerful in opening the doors to new opportunities as opposed to its underling the "dot," which closes the doors to potentially helpful pathways.

The Assumpt! serves the same purpose. By virtue of raising your assumption from the subconscious to the conscious, you now have the opportunity, if you choose, to question your thought.

In other words, the "?" symbolizes the Assumpt!, the act of surfacing your assumption, which automatically creates a pause before you follow it.

Unfortunately, while the "?" has incredible strength to stop us from moving in the wrong direction and to provoke us to explore other directions, it falls short of delivering us the complete package; it raises the question but doesn't always propel us to the answer or solution.

That responsibility for closing the deal falls on the "!" The exclamation mark is your ultimate goal. It appears at special moments, like the Wow! factor that is the end game for companies looking to spark customer or employee loyalty or the great Aha! that is your reward for finding the sought-after solution to an insurmountable problem. In simplified Chinese, the word for exclamation point, 感叹号 (pronounced *gǎntànhào*), combines the characters for emotion and admiration. That too has a celebratory feel.

The "!" represents the universal self-gratification resulting from challenging your Assumpts! It's the feeling generated when you place the last piece in the ten thousand piece puzzle or say something clever that turns a child's tears into a smile of sunshine. It's also the radiant pleasure of closing a sale, the level of deep satisfaction generated when successfully engaging an employee, the insurmountable pride of starting up your own company, or the financial rewards of creating a whole new beverage category.

Punctuation in Action

Consider light beers. Before 1975, this category of low-calorie beers did not exist.[2] In fact, a biochemist and one of the greatest influencers of today's microbreweries introduced a low-calorie diet beer in 1967.[3] Dr. Joseph Owades, the inventor of this light beer, found a way to make the enzymes in beer absorb more of the starch, which translated to fewer calories. But at that time, beer drinkers were not interested in being labeled as "watching their diets." It wasn't a macho concept, so the product never sold.

Diet beers don't work became an industry assumption.

Less than ten years later, Miller beer acquired another brewery and inherited Dr. Joseph Owades's formula. This time, the timing was right as Miller was looking for ways to expand its brand. Imagine being in the meeting to discuss the idea of introducing a light beer and having someone say, "It was tried before, and it didn't work. Period." If that conversation ended at the ".", Miller and the entire light beer industry might not exist today.

Instead, someone decided to add the "?" and radically changed the future of beer manufacturing and selling. For example, instead of investing in the assumptions that "it was tried before, and it didn't work" or "light beer isn't macho," these statements became questions, or Assumpts!, and were brought to the surface. The "?" opened the door to an exploration of ways to build a light beer business. The overall underlying assumption that "they had tried to sell light beer to the masses, and it didn't work" was now surfaced and new thinking entertained.

As will be discussed, not all assumptions or Assumpts! warrant challenging. But rapid changes in the economy, technology, and workforce foster a growing dependency on using assumptions to keep up and adapt, and this can be quite dangerous. On the flip side, the more you can successfully manage your assumptions, the greater the chance to minimize investing in dangerous ones and the greater the opportunity to turn them into assets that work for you.

That's what happened with Miller.

Miller challenged the Assumpt! that men wouldn't drink a diet beer. In essence, the Miller team went from A. No one drinks diet beers "." to B. What if we could create a diet beer market "?" to C. We can make men love a diet beer "!" Miller's solution in the late seventies was to position the product called lite beer (their spelling) as something with fewer calories that also tastes great. To make this position acceptable to men, they introduced a brilliant, humorous, and award-winning TV campaign that had well-known NFL football players, coaches, and even professional referees arguing over the benefits of drinking light beer; some said less calories, and others said great taste. The marketing presented drinking light beer as both macho and acceptable.

Challenging the Assumpt! that light beers don't sell was truly recognized in 1992 when the light beer category, which included Miller, Bud, and other breweries, surpassed all other categories in domestic beer sales in the United States.[4] That momentum continues today with the popularity of brands like Miller Lite and Bud Light. Results like this is what earns the Assumpt! the "!" But it never would have happened if the assumption "We tried it once before, and it didn't work "." went unchecked.

The Assumpt! process simply takes you from the "." to the "?" to the "!" It's a great way to simulate thinking differently and to punctuate your success. The key question now is how and when do you *challenge* your Assumpts!?

CHAPTER 8

Challenging Your Assumpts!

What is as frustrating as making a dangerous assumption? Making an Assumpt! and not knowing what to do with it. This chapter provides the guidelines for managing your Assumpts! You'll explore when to accept an Assumpt! and move on versus when to challenge and investigate it. And if you choose to challenge your Assumpt!, this chapter offers the tools that unlock closed doors, so you can step into a whole new set of opportunities you never imagined.

Turning Your Assumpts! On or Off

The binary code that makes up the DNA of all computer processing is quite simple. You have a *bit* of either 0 or 1. It's the combination of how bits are strung together that determines a letter or number. This string is called a *byte*. For example, a byte of 10100 equals the number 20.

Each bit also acts as a switch in which 0 is "off" and 1 is "on." The combination of these bits directs the flow of electricity in, say, a silicon chip; that flow is called *data*. In the early days of using bits in electric relays, bits were considered either "open" or "closed." These are terms I will reference shortly.

I am going to oversimplify things with the metaphor that Assumpts! are like bits and bytes. How you manage each Assumpt!, just like bits, determines the outcome. And how you string these Assumpts! together, like bytes, determines the flow of success or failure.

The word *closed* in relationship to managing your Assumpts! is somewhat negative as not all Assumpts! are dangerous. So, rather than think of your Assumpts! as bits that are open or closed, think of them as *checked* or *unchecked*. Choosing one of these two approaches is your first step in determining how to manage your Assumpt!

For example, in a new business plan, you make a number of Assumpts! regarding budgets, personnel, and schedules. Suppose you are presented with a plan in which every team member agrees that the production cycle for the new product is eighteen months, even though the competition is launching a similar product a few months earlier. You fear that getting a later start than your competitor will put your product at a disadvantage. You decide this time frame is an Assumpt! worth challenging and ask the group what would happen if they produce the product in twelve months. Even if they say this is impossible, you encourage them to reject the Assumpt! This forces them to think completely differently about the production process and consider ideas they may have tossed out or not considered. But it all started by getting them to "check" their Assumpt!

Now, let's say that your team provides a profile of who the next hire should be to help execute the plan. You could question this Assumpt!, but you need to get this person on board right away, and noodling the description will only slow down the process. So you keep the Assumpt! "unchecked."

The point is that managing your Assumpts! begins by deciding how much energy to invest in dissecting or accepting each one. Sometimes, it makes sense to examine the Assumpt! in more detail. Other times, it doesn't, and it's worth just moving on.

A nice way to summarize this is with the story of a friend taking me to a wonderful establishment in Santa Barbara, California. We ate at the bar, giving us a view of the entire restaurant. The food was delicious, but the service was outstanding. It was a small place, yet the staff operated seamlessly, silently weaving in and out of tables in unison to serve and clear, friendly and efficient in making sure you had what you needed.

My friend knew the owners, a husband-and-wife team, and introduced me to the wife who ran the front of the room. I complimented her on the staff and asked how she managed them so well.

"I am their mother," she said. "They come to me with all of their problems, and I help sort them out." I asked for her secret, and she told me, "When they come to me in hysterics, I say to them, 'Are we talking about a nuclear disaster or an issue over a parking space'?"

Since then, I have used her question to help me decide when it's worth investing in my Assumpts! For example, when I decide that's it's a potential "nuclear disaster," such as an Assumpt! that is guiding me to close a new business deal, then I check that Assumpt! But if it's just a "parking-space" issue, such as replying to a friend's email, then I ignore my Assumpt! that my email is not as well written as I'd like. In other words, my Assumpt! stays unchecked, and I send the email.

The process for checking your Assumpts! will be described shortly. For now, let's look at additional guidelines serving as criteria for when to check or uncheck your Assumpts!

When to Check Your Assumpts!

- **You're Stuck:** You feel like you have tried everything to solve a particular problem, but nothing seems to be working. For example, you have tried everything to get someone to respond to your email, yet still no response. Now, you feel totally hopeless. This is an ideal time to identify your Assumpts! that the content of the email is wrong or that the person who is not responding is just blowing you off. If you leave these Assumpts! unchecked, then your actions are frozen. On the other hand, checking your Assumpts! may open up new doors. Perhaps doing so will lead you in a different direction, such as picking up the phone and calling. This alternative feels so simple, yet often when we get focused on our Assumpts! without checking them, we only look at the small part of the puzzle rather than the big picture.

- **You're Dealing with Change:** Change is hard and breeds a number of assumptions that act as barriers to doing things differently. During a time of transition, it's easy to drum up all kinds of reasons why making a change won't work. For example, you have been pulled into a new project without warning and have a ton of reasons why you aren't the right person to take over. When this happens to you, it's time to check your Assumpts! as you might discover that the new responsibilities tap into talents you have that are not being used.

- **You Know There Are Expectations:** You know that if you do certain things, they will result in negative outcomes. For example, if you are under a lot of pressure and someone asks you a question, you know that if you answer during a moment of tension, it will only create more tension. This is a good time to check your Assumpts! to help you better frame your immediate response or help you decide whether to delay the answer.

- **You're Questioning the Outcome:** When you're not sure if what you're doing is actually going to work, it's a good time to check your Assumpts! For example, say you are proposing a new system to your board of directors. You know that if this system works, it will benefit the company. But it hasn't been tried yet, and you are concerned about a negative outcome. Checking your Assumpts! can help separate the reality of the outcome from the fear of presenting something totally new.

- **You're Afraid:** Have you ever been in the position of not being able to make a decision or take action? You feel frozen from the fear of making a mistake? Some people have this happen when they need to choose a paint color while others freeze when having to recommend a specific course of action or take a firm stand. One of the best ways to thaw out in these circumstances is to check the Assumpts! blocking your ability to make a decision. Many people assume that if they make a mistake, they will be fired. This is a dangerous Assumpt! that often permeates an organization, and when it goes unchecked, it's responsible for that organization's inability to change.

When to Leave Your Assumpts! Unchecked

In some situations, however, leaving your Assumpts! unchecked is the best move. As mentioned earlier, many of your assumptions serve you very well, leading to positive outcomes. Also, as discussed, examining every assumption is not practical. Here are some guidelines for when to leave your Assumpts! unchecked:

- **It's Not Worth It:** You are at the supermarket checkout, and the item being rung up is two cents more than you remember it being priced when you pulled it off the shelf. Your Assumpt! is that you are right. But you are late for a meeting, and you don't really want to wait for the checkout clerk to go back into the store to confirm the price. So you leave this Assumpt! unchecked.

- **It Would Stop Momentum:** Determining when something is "complete" is really an assumption. For some people, it means getting whatever you are working on 100 percent correct. For others, "complete" is a matter of getting it out the door. Nitpicking the details will only kill the momentum. Just consider when a new operating system or software is released. There are always issues that get corrected over time because it's cheaper to go to market now than hold the product back until it's close to perfect. Sometimes, when momentum is more important than the "just-right" outcome, it's time to leave your Assumpts! unchecked.

- **You Accept the Consequences:** You want to tell someone he or she is not doing the proper share of work. This person has a volatile personality and may become defensive and angry regardless of your approach. But you don't care about the individual's response and therefore leave your Assumpts! unchecked.

Challenging Your Assumpts!

Once you say or think, "My Assumpt! is . . . " and decide to check it, it's now time to challenge it. Challenging your Assumpts! gives you permission to explore alternative ideas (new ways of doing things), entertain possibilities that you did not think existed, and uncover new opportunities. Challenging your Assumpts! also provides you with an ability to make smarter decisions because you manage your assumptions instead of them managing you. You will minimize having to say after a disappointing product launch, "I guess I shouldn't have assumed that everyone would love my product." Instead, you will celebrate your product launch, remembering the decisions you made after you said, "My Assumpt! was that everyone loves my product. But when I challenged it, look at what I discovered."

The ultimate goal of challenging your Assumpts! is to help you look into a mirror and see something completely different looking back at you. What you see could be a different way of processing a payment, positioning your company, talking to an employee, or generating a strategy. The possibilities and alternatives are endless.

As wonderful as these outcomes may sound, not everyone believes they will benefit from this process. For instance, the senior leader of a financial services company trying to find new ways to drive revenue confessed that he was "a banker, not an innovator." He did not believe he had the ability to truly think differently. But we all do.

More often than not, we are the ones who hold ourselves back from generating innovative ideas. And the restraints we put on ourselves begin with our comfort level in stepping out of the box.

Understanding Your Comfort Zone

In some of my workshops I share an exercise in which a group is asked to figure out how a magic trick is done by challenging their Assumpts! It's wonderful to watch people dive into the problem, explore ideas they had never considered, and then collectively find the solution.

During one such exercise, I noticed a woman taking pictures of everyone rather than sitting with a group. I purposely inquired what she was doing because of my own Assumpt! that she might be avoiding participation. The woman told me she was in human resources and was documenting the experience. Then she added, "Besides, I am not good at these types of things."

How often have we said similar words when trying to do something we have never done before? It could be learning a new software program, moving into a new business group, being forced to change to a new accounting system, or being asked to run a meeting.

The woman taking the photos at the session was probably quite competent in solving human resources issues, but when it came to tackling the solution to a magic trick, she assumed the answers were beyond her reach. This has nothing to do with talent or ability. Her *assumptions* held her back. The reason I know this is that when I got her to sit down, join the group, and challenge her Assumpt!, something truly magical happened. Within thirty seconds, she had figured out how the trick was done. I've conducted this exercise hundreds of times and have never seen someone figure out the answer so fast.

The Magician's Assistant

Note: *This exercise is to be done as a group. If you're interested in employing this exercise, contact me at andy@andycohen.com, and I will share the secret of how it's done.*

At one point in my seminars, I use magic as a metaphor to teach the Assumpt! Magic works because it's engaging, and as one participant told me, "Sometimes when I forget the message, I can recall the illusion, and it all comes back."

In this form of magic, titled "The Magician's Assistant," I gather up to sixty participants around a large table with a deck of cards placed in the center. Someone in the group is randomly selected to pick up the deck, examine it, shuffle it, and then pull out nine cards to be placed faceup on the table.

One of the participants is then introduced as my "assistant" and asked to leave the room. Next, a randomly chosen participant points and singles out a faced-up card on the table. The assistant comes back, studies the room, studies the cards, reads everyone's energy, and correctly identifies that card. Every time.

We do the trick twice to prove it isn't a fluke. Then, I turn to someone in the crowd and ask this person to take over the role of the assistant. Normally, this request is met with a blank stare or a look of panic as the individual thinks, "I'm in trouble. No way. Can't be done. I don't know the secret." I explain to everyone that these are the typical assumptions we make in business: we don't think we can accomplish a certain task, feel we lack the knowledge to move forward, or are afraid because we have never done something before. These are all common business situations that move us out of our comfort zones everyday.

But when you leave these assumptions unchecked, you automatically bar yourself from reaching your desired goals.

So I ask the group to check their assumptions related to figuring out how the magic trick is done. They are encouraged to identify those assumptions, turn them into Assumpts!, and then question or reject them.

In giving yourself permission to challenge your assumptions, you are giving yourself permission to think differently.

The large group breaks into smaller groups to discuss how they think the trick was accomplished. They begin collaborating to craft real possibilities. They discuss that I might be using words to signal the location, or my head, legs, eyes, or hand. They suggest that I might be using a smartphone to take a picture of the selected card and then transmit it. They explore the idea that the group gives away the card by subconsciously looking at it. In a perfect world, we would have a video camera that tapes the trick so that the group could test those Assumpts! But we don't, so instead they have to challenge each one to test its plausibility through discussion.

The key for the group is to leverage their Assumpts! in a way that provides them with options that did not exist moments before. Challenging their Assumpts! automatically provides permission to think differently.

After ten minutes of discussion, everyone reconvenes, and the Assumpts! are shared and written out on a whiteboard. We then explore each Assumpt! and decide if it stays on the board or gets crossed out.

Everyone is then invited to come back to the table as the trick is repeated. This time they have a library of Assumpts! to refer to, and as they watch the trick, the answer begins to appear. Just like magic, face after face begins to light up with the recognition that they now know the secret.

Fifteen minutes ago, the participants assumed they couldn't think like magicians. Now, they've discovered the trick all on their own. That's the power of challenging your Assumpts!

Moving Out of Your Comfort Zone

We're all at a certain point uncomfortable changing our behavior or beliefs. It is at this point that we generate a number of assumptions that act as barriers to thinking or doing things differently.

Early in my career, I decided to invent a new type of salad dressing. After working a full day, I would come home and work on this project. I knew nothing about creating or manufacturing a food product but believed I had a great salad-dressing concept. Within a year, I was rewarded with the experience of presenting the idea to a variety of packaged-goods companies. But in the early days of development when I was starting from scratch, I was amazed at how my mind would "lie" to me when it came time to sit down and do the work. It would say things like:

- "You're an idiot for doing this."

- "You could be with your friends right now having a good time."

- "This will never get off the ground."

- "You've already invested too much time in this."

I discovered that the growing number of reasons why I shouldn't pursue the idea grew in proportion to the anxiety I was feeling in trying to work out an idea in an area I was not familiar with. What made this so clear was that during the same day, I had no trouble spewing out ideas for a new TV campaign for one of my clients, as this was something I was comfortable doing. But creating ideas for a product of my own in an area that was new to me was a struggle.

People's comfort zones are unique. Salespeople, for instance, are comfortable putting themselves in new situations, facing the unknown. Going into a room and speaking with strangers in order to make a sale isn't a big deal. But give those salespeople a new software program for detailing expenses, and they'll likely begin to sweat.

Aron Ralston, a hiker who became famous for severing his own arm after it got stuck between two rocks, admitted in a morning-show interview that his greatest fear in going to the hospital was having to get a shot. Needles made him uncomfortable.[1]

Houdini was the king of escapes—nothing could hold him back. Yet when riding with a friend in a newly modeled car, he couldn't open the door on his own because the door handle was in a different place than older models. Joked Houdini, "I've escaped from practically every type of a container and every size, shape, and weight of boxes, trunks, and other such things, but I wish someone would tell me how I can get out of this darned automobile!"[2]

Orville Wright, one of the two brothers who ushered in the art of modern aviation by inventing and flying the first plane, dismissed the idea of creating a runway that smoothed over the rocks and debris on the airfield. In his eyes, if a man had to smooth over every takeoff strip (which today is called a tarmac), he shouldn't be flying.[3]

We all have our own range of comfort zones we operate in. Venturing outside the zone generates anxiety and doubts. Sometimes, we tolerate this level of discomfort. Many times, we do not.

Yet today's disruptive business world demands that you change and adapt, or perish. Everything is in a state of flux: your job, technology, the economy, and the workforce. The good part is that you are not alone. It is quite common to assume that it's "only you" who is having the problem adapting, working through the problem, or struggling to find new options.

But when it comes to doing things differently, thinking differently, and changing, we are all in it together. It's hard work.

The point I am making is that for many people, challenging Assumpts! can generate a level of anxiety driven by moving out of our comfort zones. A banker exploring thinking differently may be as uncomfortable in the effort as an innovator exploring tough financial decisions.

It's important to remember how easy it is for your assumptions to fester during a time of change. This is why I have created a number of strategies for challenging Assumpts! that range from risk-free to riskier. You will discover that each of these strategies has its own merits and can be used by itself or in conjunction with others. You will identify with some of them. Others will feel a bit foreign. I encourage you to try them all because you never know where they will take you.

I've summarized these strategies to make them easier for you to digest. Afterwards, I will share specific case histories illustrating some of these particular strategies.

Risk-Free Ways to Challenge Your Assumpts!

Risk-free challenges require nothing more than reflecting on your Assumpts! There is no downside to this as you are evolving a thought as opposed to radically changing your mindset.

Verify and Probe for More Information

This is so simple and obvious, yet it's surprising how often people ignore this strategy. We skim emails, the web, and news on TV. Our pace of life has so significantly picked up that taking the time to read something in detail has become a luxury. The Internet allows anyone to publish, and when what they post shows up on the top-third of your search engine, there is a tendency to treat it as truth. Over the next twenty-four hours, observe what you say to others, and explore where that information came from. Ask yourself how confident you are that this information is true. When others state something that sounds like an Assumpt!, ask them to share their sources. I think you will find a number of Assumpts! worth challenging.

The point is that when you make an Assumpt!, take five minutes and seek to verify it. This is an easy way to challenge with no expenditure except a short period of time. My Assumpt! is that the information you will discover in doing this simple exercise will have a much longer shelf life than the time you took to verify it.

Ask a Question

This strategy is a bit different than "verify and probe" as it focuses on a different outcome. Asking a question allows you to consider options without pushing yourself outside of your comfort zone. For example, as senior leader you are frustrated with the behavior of your team members. They work hard but don't prioritize. The problems you discuss with them always seem to become the ones they immediately focus on. This causes a pileup as nothing gets completed, only started. Your Assumpt! is that the only way to change this is for you to assign priorities. But this isn't practical. Your group needs a level of autonomy so that they can switch priorities based on their own workflow and schedules. So you look at your Assumpt! and use the "What if?" question. You say, "What if I ask them to set the priorities and then give them feedback?" Asking this type of question opens the doors to doing things a bit differently and receiving the results you want to achieve.

You can use "Perhaps if we tried . . . " the same way: "Perhaps if we tried having them discuss what they feel are the most important issues, then I would get a sense of where their priorities lie. This way, we can explore if we are in alignment."

Make Yourself a Part of the Act

A good strategy to use when you are anxious is to "act as if." This means that if you are extremely nervous about making a presentation, then act as if you aren't nervous. The point is that if you give in to the anxieties, you will never give yourself the chance to discover what is on the other side. Often, when you "act as if," you discover that your reasons to be nervous have no foundation or that your anxieties haven't stopped you from giving a great presentation.

Adam Grant, writer of *Give and Take: Why Helping Others Drives Our Success*, is an engaging speaker as well as a best-selling author. Yet Grant admits that he is really an introvert who decided to act like an extrovert when he first began public speaking.[4] Making believe you are good at what you want to do is a wonderful way to discover all the positive energy that results when you cross over to the other side of your comfort zone. For example, if you get a job promotion that requires taking on a leadership role, act as if you are a leader—even though you might want to run and hide.

You can draw a parallel with challenging your Assumpt! in order to establish a focused goal that changes the company. Doing so might generate what business author Jim Collins calls BHAGs: big hairy audacious goals.[5] These are goals that appear extremely questionable but perhaps doable. Often, BHAGs generated from challenging Assumpts! are often immediately dismissed as no good, too far out, or something no one will buy into.

Rather than toss out an idea, I encourage those who are uncomfortable with the idea to make it a part of the act. If you are one of those people, try saying to yourself, "I will act like it's a good idea. Now, how can I contribute to it?" This simple thought gives you permission to safely entertain this idea and allow more time to play it out without committing to it. Also, by owning part of the idea by contributing to it, you will be more motivated to explore it.

Suspend Judgment

Next time someone suggests an idea and you immediately label it as "bad," it's time to suspend judgment of your Assumpt! This has nothing to do with being right or wrong. Rather, it's about cutting off a path that has the potential to lead to new places. For example, I have been presented with a number of ideas for enhancing my business but found myself first judging them as "stupid," "ignorant of the issues," or "just bad ideas." Later, I often discover that if I had taken the time to identify and challenge these Assumpts!, I would have profited from the comments' merits.

My Assumpt! is that you have experience using similar words about your own ideas or those of others. This is why I suggest using a phrase like this: "I don't agree, but that's not important right now. Let's look at it your way." This lets the person know where you stand while providing him or her the opportunity to demonstrate the idea's value. In essence, you suspend your Assumpt! and allow others to challenge it.

Seek Alignment

Communication is mostly nonverbal. People's manners, tone of conversation, and facial expressions add much of the meaning to conversations. Therefore, modes like texts and emails often put us at a disadvantage in understanding a person's meaning. This is one of the reasons those smiling faces called *emojis* are so popular, for they add emotion to online communications. This doesn't dismiss the value and functionality of these forms of communication, but it does raise a red flag that the less personal contact you have in a discussion, the more you have to interpret what is being said. This results in generating a number of Assumpts!

An easy way to compensate for interpreting messages the wrong way is to seek alignment. For example, if I send someone an email regarding a meeting tomorrow, I will write, "tomorrow, Monday." This eliminates the chance of the recipient reading the email the next day and assuming "Tuesday."

In conversations in which the details are important and you want to minimize any Assumpts! being made, I propose you say, "Let me repeat what you just told me to make sure I am hearing it as you mean it." This is a very effective and risk-free way of making sure your Assumpts! are in alignment with theirs.

But fair warning, people move so quickly in today's business world that they often get a bit angry when you ask to align Assumpts! Their assumption is that you are slowing things down and what they said (or you said) is perfectly clear. Don't give up. What you receive in small irritations is nothing compared to the bigger irritations that follow when the Assumpts! conflict or clash.

Riskier Ways to Challenge Your Assumpts!

Write Your Own Script

In Chapter 4, I introduced the strategy of "writing your own script," including examples that demonstrate how it helps you turn a "no" into a "yes." Now, let's reexplore this strategy with broader-range examples.

When great artists "write their own script, they violate the expected norms to create something no one ever imagined. Consider the evolution in painting of the twentieth century: Fauvism, Expressionism, Cubism, Abstraction, Dada, and Surrealism. Each style broke from past traditions to create a new art form.

These artists asked the question, "Who said it had to be this way?"

The reason this strategy is risky is because it quickly moves you out of your comfort zone with a more aggressive question than "What if?" "Who said it has to be this way?" forces you to question traditional processes and even existing cultures. Remember, an organization's culture is the sum of its aligned assumptions. To question these assumptions means threatening the culture.

It's less risky to apply this strategy to yourself. For example, a young teacher asked me if she could start a school for children if she has no money. Her Assumpt! was that money was the issue. I encouraged her to *write her own script* so that money wasn't an issue. We then began discussing her unique style of teaching, ways of finding an existing school that aligned with her style, the possibilities of helping to run the organization, how to build her own brand along the way, and then getting backers to support her vision for a school.

This sounds like common sense. But when you are stuck behind your Assumpt!, your vision gets impaired, and common sense goes out the door. Again, that's why you need to challenge your Assumpts!

Think on the Other Side of the Box

When you look at a box, you think you see the whole box. But generally, you only see four or five sides, not six. Think of that sixth side as the other person's perspective and invisible thoughts. The sixth side could be the color red, or transparent, or missing completely. As Figure 5 suggests, you just don't know until you look or validate.

So if you were to insist that the box was all blue or completely solid, you would be mistaken. And that could be costly because you are assuming you know what is on the other side. One of the greatest gifts in life is to be able to step into someone's shoes and look at the world from his or her viewpoint. If you want to save yourself time marketing a product, increase your success in motivating an employee, or sell your strategy up the line, try challenging the Assumpt! that "the world thinks the same way as me" by thinking on the other side of the box. This will be discussed in more detail in Part 3 and the chapter on Benjamin Bach (Chapter 9).

The key to remember is that you see the world through your eyes. Your Assumpts! are based on what *you* feel, learn, experience, etc. Seeing the world through the other person's perspective increases the odds that what you are offering the person or trying to get him or her to do has a greater chance of acceptance.

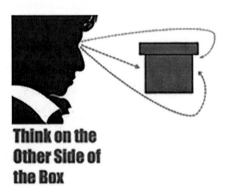

Think on the Other Side of the Box

Figure 5. View the situation from all sides, not just the sides you see.

Reject Everything

Dr. Amar Bose, who passed away in 2013, was the founder of the Bose Corporation.[5] He created the famous Bose radio, reengineered how sound was heard, and even found a way to improve the driving experience. He was famous for getting excited when one of his engineers said, "it can't be done" as Dr. Bose wouldn't take "no" for an answer. Steve Jobs shared the same trait and had little tolerance for those who would explain why something couldn't happen when he wanted it to happen.

We label people like these visionaries. My Assumpt! is that we are all visionaries if we give ourselves the chance to reject our Assumpts! Rejecting your Assumpts! is the fastest way to generate new and innovative ideas, break through old habits, or change the way things are traditionally done.

It's quite inspiring when this happens. Take Corporal Todd Love, a third-generation Marine, who became a triple amputee after stepping on an improvised explosive device (IED) while serving in Afghanistan in 2010. Most of us would assume that our lives would be limited by this handicap. While Love does admit life isn't easy, he rejects the assumption that his condition will stop him from living an adventurous life. So he learned how to surf on his hands as well as ski, wrestle with alligators, and compete in challenging Spartan Races.[7]

Operation Surf[8] was cofounded when wounded Navy Corpsman Derek McGuiness, who lost his leg, decided he wanted to surf. This weeklong program gives wounded vets, many who lost legs and hands, the chance to do something they didn't think possible: learn surfing and, in turn, regain confidence. Said Van Curaza, who helped establish Operation Surf, "By the end of the week, they're just lit up. When they ride that wave, they are badass."[9]

When it comes to rejecting assumptions and doing revolutionary things in business, Dr. Bose's work with automobiles is a great illustration.[10] In the past fifty years, auto manufacturers have focused on how to make car suspensions better. Suspension systems are the link between a car and its wheels. They serve dual purposes: safety in the way the car handles turns (brakes) and comfort in reducing bumps and vibrations. But improving handling at the same time as comfort is often at odds. So the focus has been on finding the balance by improving fluid-based suspension hardware.

Dr. Bose, however, decided to reject the industry hardware assumption that handling and ride couldn't be improved at the same time. In 1980, he began exploring how to optimize these two opposing goals. This led him to create a unique electromagnetic suspension system for cars that is void of fluids. As the Bose Corporation describes, "The Bose suspension system includes a linear electromagnetic motor and power amplifier at each wheel and a set of control algorithms. This proprietary combination of suspension hardware and control software makes it possible, for the first time, to combine superior comfort and superior control in the same vehicle."[11]

This innovative suspension system has been tested in a Lexus and is being explored by auto manufacturers as a way to revolutionize the riding experience. Today, this innovative system is being utilized in big-rig seats as it moves through hyperspace on its journey into the everyday car. When will it get there? A date hasn't been set, but watching this product evolve is proving to be a very exciting ride.

Challenging Assumpts! Case Histories

Here are three case histories that further illustrate the strategies for challenging your Assumpts! Please note that I have taken the liberty to incorporate the term *Assumpt!* to reflect its usage and application. I don't want to represent that these companies used the term as it was introduced after these business decisions were made.

Amazon: Encouraging Your Customers to Use Your Competitors

Introducing your customers to competitors offering a lower price is a crazy idea, yet that is exactly what Amazon did. In 2000 and in the absence of any supporting research, Jeff Bezos, founder of Amazon, invited third-party vendors to sell their goods through Amazon, even when they offered a low price. Bezos recognized the Assumpt! that it might significantly cannibalize profits, but he felt that offering third-party goods for less than what Amazon offered reinforced Amazon's commitment that the customer comes first.

Space on a web page has value in the same way as real estate. Amazon was not only advertising its competitors but also giving up valuable property to them. Imagine a retail bank offering to help you get the best mortgage even if it's with another bank. Or an automotive company showing you the best car even if it's not on its lot. It wouldn't happen, right?

In rejecting the concept of keeping your competition away from your customers, Amazon brought its customer to the competition. But instead of losing a sale to a lower price, Amazon discovered that in the long run, it's more profitable making a few pennies in commission by connecting its customers to the best prices rather than risk losing them to that best price.

In 2014, Amazon revealed that it now had two million third-party vendors on its site, producing record sales of over two billion units.[12]

Amazon redefined the customer shopping experience by rejecting the Assumpt! that directing customers to a competitor's lower price would cannibalize long-term sales. What makes this idea more admirable is that Amazon had no data that would support the profitability of the idea. It was not measurable at that time.

So ask yourself, What do your customers want that would make them happy but potentially reduce your revenue? What are the assumptions you come up with? Now, turn them into Assumpts! and challenge them using any of the strategies you've learned. Give yourself permission to explore without judgment.

HSBC Bank: Banking on Unbankable Customers

At one time, getting a banking account as a national immigrant was very difficult in the UK. And without a banking account, you couldn't get a credit card or cell phone account. This made life quite difficult for those moving to the UK from another country. Three major assumptions drove this banking access restriction: many foreign nationalists were not creditworthy, lacked a good education, and were unbankable (not profitable).

HSBC Bank recognized these assumptions and turned them into Assumpts!, adopting multiple strategies to challenge them HSBC looked to verify the Assumpt! regarding education level and discovered the opposite: in 2004, 20 percent of UK immigrants had university degrees as opposed to 17 percent of the UK-born population.[13] Through verification, the corporation also challenged the bankability assumption and realized that immigrants had over time proven to demonstrate significant wealth and entrepreneurship.

HSBC then asked the question, "What if we provide them with an account? What would it look like?" This gave HSBC permission to play with ideas in offering a new type of service that met the needs of a group moving to a new country without having a residential address while at the same time addressing the concern of creditability.

Finally, HSBC rejected the assumption of the traditional banking model and developed a combination banking and relocation service called Passport. This service required a small monthly fee with a year's commitment to keeping the account open. Once the account was set up, HSBC showed customers how to acquire a debit card, receive cell phone service, and, most importantly, build credit. HSBC even set up customer service centers with staff who spoke multiple languages to make it more comfortable for prospects to ask their questions about banking and relocating.

Within the first year, HSBC captured 5 percent of this market that had always existed but was not tapped into. Within three years, it had 33 percent of that market.[14] It was like picking low-hanging fruit that brought hundreds of thousands of new dollars into the bank and at the same time provided an invaluable service to an untapped and valuable customer base. In May 2007, HSBC reported attracting 43K new customers from over 200 different nationalities since Passport's June 2006 launch.[15]

The company also reported that the average Passport account was more profitable than the average Basic bank account and helped to enhance HSBC's global image while providing upgrade and cross-selling opportunities.

That's one of the wonderful things about challenging Assumpts! It's an opportunity to provide a win-win situation for everyone by turning a negative situation into a positive one.

Sometimes, it's as simple as asking yourself questions that may make you uncomfortable. Questions such as, "What if we change the entire customer experience? How can we do it differently than what others in our industry are doing?" Let your answers guide you out of your comfort zones into new perspectives and new opportunities, which may prove to be extremely valuable.

The Grateful Dead: How Being Dead Wrong Was Right
In the early 1980s, the first music compact disc (CD) was released. This digitized format turned out to be a golden age for the music business as it generated high profit margins while stimulating new royalties as people abandoned their vinyl records to enjoy this new

technology. The idea of giving your music away free was bad business.

Yet, during the 1980s, one music group challenged the Assumpt! that allowing people to freely record your music was a deadly business model. Instead, this group invited their fans to steal their music. The Grateful Dead set up recording zones at their live concerts so that people could record and share music. By rejecting the Assumpt! that you receive royalty on every song, the Grateful Dead expanded their customer base, sustained loyal listeners, and stimulated attendance at their live concerts. Thirty-five years later, the Dead turned out to be visionaries as the profitability in music is now driven by live concerts as paid record sales dwindle.

Ask yourself what assumptions are driven by the way your industry does business. Turn your answers into Assumpts!, and then reject them. There is a good chance the majority may be too unrealistic. But you need only one good new idea to change the way you do business and drive profits.

PART 3

Everyday Assumpts! to Challenge

As this book demonstrates, I put my own behavior under the microscope with the intent of turning my personal assumptions into business and life lessons. I also believe that each of us has his or her own story that converts into a lecture we can all learn from.

My degree in experimental psychology trained me to do my best to keep things empirical; this is why I always include research and case studies supporting my points.

My theories are based on real-time observations and results. My days in direct marketing taught me how people think. Prospects read a piece of advertising copy or watch a commercial and respond by making an inquiry or purchasing a product, or they don't. This type of real-world feedback provides a window to how people react and why.

When I began to give keynotes, I learned to watch the audience. Their responses showed me which ideas excited them and which put them to sleep. Listening to their questions during seminars provided the insights on which personal lessons resonated and which had little meaning.

But people's personal stories serve as my most enjoyable lessons about business and life. This is why Part 3 is my favorite section of this book. My Assumpt! is that every person has a story that contains a life lesson to benefit us all. I have learned over time that the more I share my stories with others, the more they want to share theirs.

This is a gift, because when people unwrap part of their lives, I learn something new that I can with their permission share with others. My global travels enrich the collection of these stories by demonstrating how uniquely different cultures are yet how amazingly similar our thoughts and assumptions can be.

It is my treat to share what I have learned with you.

CHAPTER 9

Doesn't Everyone Think Like That?

Humans are like snowflakes. No two are exactly alike. And yet we tend to forget that. For example, have you ever gotten angry with someone who "didn't do it the same way you would have"? Or, have you ever been frustrated at someone who doesn't understand something even though it's "clear to you"? It's perfectly natural to assume that the world thinks like you, but this assumption is quite dangerous when left unchecked because it often creates unrealistic expectations and keeps you from understanding what motivates an employee or consumer.

This chapter is designed to help you understand how the assumption that everyone thinks like you do filters your perceptions and often misdirects your thinking. Once you gain that understanding, it is easier to create more positive outcomes.

Behind the Scenes: My Bus Ride with Benjamin Bach

I met Benjamin Bach, a managing director for 20th Century Fox, on a bus ride to the Madame Tussauds wax museum in Los Angeles. Earlier that afternoon, I had spoken to Bach and his peers at a global marketing conference for 20th Century Fox. Now I was being bussed to a dinner party held at this famous landmark, and fortune had me sitting next to Bach who revealed a very personal assumption that we can all learn and benefit from.[1]

Everyone Can Hear Colors, Right?

Christmas dinner is a special time that brings a family together. For Benjamin Bach, however, Christmas dinner was the time he discovered he was different than others. The path to this discovery took thirty-five years.

After university, Bach left his family and friends in Cologne, Germany, and started his career stocking supermarket shelves for a European grocery chain in Ireland. His talent as a problem solver was quickly recognized, however, and he moved into a supervisory role. He then received a company car, a clear sign he was on his way up the corporate ladder. But one day his friend told him of an opportunity to work as a personal assistant on a film being shot in London. Bach, having a secret love for the film industry, packed his bags, quit his job, and began working on a movie set for very little pay.

Now, Bach is a managing director for 20th Century Fox, a role that requires an assortment of talents: salesmanship, analytics, marketing, and a bit of charm. He uses his combination of these talents to persuade movie theater chains to show the films produced by 20th Century Fox and to support these movies' extensive marketing campaigns.

Figure 6. Benjamin Bach and his superpower
(photo courtesy of Benjamin Bach)

Box-office numbers don't lie. Bach is under pressure everyday to deliver, so naturally, he looks for ways to relieve the steam. And though film is his passion, reading is one of his ways to escape.

So one Christmas he shared with his family a story he was reading called *A Deal with the Devil* by the Swiss author Martin Suter. The book's heroine, Sonia Frey, escapes to a remote village in the Swiss Alps to get away from a recent divorce driven by spousal abuse. As her past begins to catch up with her, she periodically hikes further into the mountains to clear her head. During these outdoor excursions, she has waves of seeing sounds and hearing colors. And at one point, she sees numbers with colors.

In relating this story at Christmas dinner, Bach made an offhand comment about what a big deal the author was making over these scenes, as if this type of neurological experience was something that no one else ever had. "I mean, anyone can do that," he said.

"No, I can't do that," said his father. "I can't do it either," replied his sister. "Nor I," said his sister's husband. And to Bach's shock, each person around the table began to admit the same thing. None of them had ever felt, tasted, or heard a color.

Bach was thirty-five years old that Christmas Day. Yet this was the first time in his life that he discovered he had a different sensory pathway. Still, he couldn't accept the fact that others did not share this ability.

So he began calling his friends to quiz them. "When you think of the number eight, what color do you see?" he would ask. "I don't see any color," replied his friends.

That's when Bach finally realized that not everyone had the same ability nor did they think the same way as him when it came to remembering a day.

The term for this neurological phenomenon is *synesthesia*. And it's a kind of superpower as it allows people to do some extraordinary things. Some people with it hear sounds and associate them with colors. Others can see an abstract object and taste a particular food. For Bach, every date in the calendar is associated with a distinct color. In essence, he feels a color around every date.

Once Bach became aware of this "talent," he realized why his friends would always include him in discussions about what happened in the past. For example, they would ask him to recall a specific date of a party years ago when X kissed Y. Bach would see a color associated with a number and respond with something like May 8, 1992.

SYNESTHESIA
0123456789

Figure 7. A neurological phenomenon in which sensory pathways cross

It's estimated that 1 to 4 percent of the world's population has synesthesia,[2] and there are synesthesia societies for people with this neurological condition to meet, share stories, and learn more about what causes it and how to enjoy living with it. If those with synesthesia join a society, they invariably find that others, too, have been completely unaware of their condition until much later in life.

Even for those of us who don't have synesthesia, the point is obvious. What we think is normal, such as seeing numbers as colors, may not be normal for everyone else. In fact, Bach confessed how frustrated and angry he became throughout his life when people couldn't remember events or what happened on certain dates. He thought they were just being lazy. This kind of thing was common and easy for him, so it must be for others as well, he assumed.

Bach and others with synesthesia remind us how easy it is to assume that "the world thinks just like me."

I Just Assumed You Understood

I am guilty of this exact sort of thing. I tend to think very fast, and it's taken me years to learn that others don't process information the same way or as quickly. Understanding this Assumpt! helps me to be more patient when discussing an idea or to not get angry when the other person requires a more detailed explanation.

At seminars, when I ask people to record assumptions they've made, one common theme often surfaces around scheduling.

As an example, two people agree to meet at 8:30 a.m. to give a new business pitch. Both show up at that time, but the other person isn't there. One went to the office assuming they would drive together to the meeting, and the other went directly to the office of the prospect. Each person saw the situation from his or her own unique perspective and assumed the other shared that perspective.

In another example, a joint conference call is set in the calendar for 10:00 a.m., but the other person doesn't call in until 1:00 p.m. The discrepancy arises because each person assumed the call was on his or her time zone. Scheduling assumptions can lead to levels of frustration and tension, such as when I got angry at my tennis partner for not showing up for the game at 8:00 a.m. when we were actually scheduled to play at 8:00 that night.

One of my favorite examples is the story of a wife who asked her husband to go shopping and provided him with a list. To make things easier for him, she numbered the items she wanted as one, two, and three—all the way up to twenty. The husband returned from shopping, and his wife couldn't believe what he did. He bought one bag of sugar, two bags of flour, and twenty bags of 20 lb. dog food. She was angered by his lack of judgment, and he was just as angry by her assuming he would understand her list.[3]

There is no right or wrong in these types of situations because each party assumes he or she understands what to do. Yet when things don't turn out as expected, each party is convinced that the other "didn't listen" or "should have known." The ability to create division between people so quickly is what makes this assumption so dangerous.

Everyone Is Going to Love This

Here is an example that shows the consequences of assuming that we all share the same heroes and interests.

Peter Thiel is a highly successful, modern-day Renaissance man. His achievements include being a cofounder of PayPal, a professor at Stanford University, a hedge-fund manager, and author (with Blake Masters) of the best-selling book written for start-ups titled *Zero to One: Notes on Startups, or How to Build the Future.* In this book, he provides a humorous illustration of how what's "cool" to you isn't necessarily "cool" to others.[4]

In PayPal's early years, the company held a press conference to introduce PayPal payments using a PalmPilot, one of the first tablet-based devices. The concept was to demonstrate how people could beam money from their PalmPilot to someone else's.

Symptoms You May Be Seeing the World through Your Eyes Only

Here are some sayings from DAD to help you quickly identify when this assumption is in play.

"Don't they get it"?

"They should have known."

"They're idiots."

"It's so obvious."

"(Sigh) I already explained it to them."

"That's not the way I would do it."

"They are just being lazy."

"Why don't they get it"!

"I couldn't have been clearer."

"I would have had it done two days ago."

"They'd never do that here."

Many of the original employees of PayPal were engineers. And they thought that Scotty from the original *Star Trek* TV show was really cool because he was also an engineer. So when they held a press conference to announce their service of digitally sending money, they assumed that engaging the actor James Doohan, the original Scotty on *Star Trek*, to kick off the event was a no-brainer. In addition, they would have him say something like, "Beam me up some money." Uttering these lines would make PayPal immortal, would drive huge press, and then definitely go viral.

Unfortunately, not everyone shared this enthusiasm. Very little of the press came, and those who did weren't at all excited when James Doohan appeared.

PayPal's choice to use Doohan as its spokesperson may have been influenced by Priceline, who two years before had successfully engaged William Shatner, the original Captain Kirk. The Priceline commercials starring Shatner had gained a lot of attention with the trade as well as consumers. Even so, Thiel admitted that he and his PayPal peers learned an important lesson: the world doesn't always think like engineers.

The power of leaving this assumption unchecked was reinforced over time as PayPal learned that in 1997, the consumer wasn't enamored with beaming money through the PalmPilot as much as they would be through the Internet (which was eventually where PayPal found its success). In other words, seeing your customer as someone just like you can be a dangerous assumption that needs to be checked and challenged.

Doesn't Everyone Think Like That?

The assumption "Doesn't everyone think like that?" is the cause of many management issues. Small business owners often assume that every employee shares the same passion as if it's his or her business too. For example, in a crisis they expect that all employees will naturally put in extra hours just as they will. But this sets up unrealistic expectations that will never be met and interferes with group harmony as the owner is always disappointed. Similarly, it's often difficult for a senior leader to understand that not every member of the group operates in the same way. For example, team leaders tend to think strategically, for they are responsible for multiple business functions and overall profits. Yet, they are often quite frustrated when teams fixate on the tactical issues.

I had the opportunity of exploring the assumption that "employees think tactically" with a group of high-level leaders at an executive seminar at Duke University's Fuqua School of Business, one of the most respected business schools in the United States. These leaders represented well-known companies in shipping, mining, transportation, utilities, and finance.

During our time together, I picked up this theme that seemed to trouble a majority of these executives. Even though they came from very different organizations, they were all complaining about their employees' tendency to think tactically rather than strategically. The more these business leaders talked about it, the more they reinforced each other's belief that employees cared only about tactics, not strategy.

I decided to challenge their collective assumption. Ten days after the course, I sent all the participants an interactive survey plus a video in which I recapped the process for challenging Assumpts! I then asked them to step back and put themselves in their employees' shoes. Specifically, I asked these executives to jot down all the assumptions their employees might be making that were driving this tactical thinking. Here are their responses, organized by categories:

Assumption 1:
Strategy Is Someone Else's Job

- Strategic plans are already decided by upper management, and I have no influence over those types of decisions.

- Their job is to carry out actions given to them by their managers who are already thinking strategically. Their only role is to execute.

- Someone else does that.

- Strategy is not part of my job description.

Assumption 2:
Incentives and Culture Do Not Encourage
Strategic Thinking

- Any idea or concept that doesn't fit into the "norm" will be dismissed or discarded without any real thought or discussion.

- There are no measurements for strategic work, so focusing on tactics is a faster and more solid path to rewards.

- Incentive schemes (for many) are geared toward tactical/short-term goals; therefore, strategic thinking is not required.

Assumption 3:
I Have No Time and No Resources
(Not a Priority)

- Operational issues are more important than strategy.

- Implementing a strategy is a long-term solution, or it cannot be done quickly enough to solve an issue requiring near-term resolution.

- I am too busy carrying out tactics to stop and think strategically.

- Tactics are what matter in this business.

- I have no visible picture of the future, which makes it impossible to think strategically.

- We don't have the time to think strategically—we have too much to get done, with too little time and resources. We just need to get our work done, and thinking about new, different, and unique ways takes away from our ability to just get the job accomplished.

Assumption 4:
I Don't Have the Authority or Ability

- I have insufficient authority to define strategy that affects other departments or divisions.

- No one will listen to my ideas.

- "My idea will not be good enough"; therefore, why bother thinking strategically?

- I don't know how to think strategically.

- We would not be able to get others on board and to go along with a different, unique, or new way of approaching a challenge, so why make the effort?

Once you take the time to understand how another person is wired differently than you, something magical happens. You begin to see the situation through his or her eyes, which allows you to share the problem. Instead of "us" versus "them," it's now "we," such as, How can "we" make this happen? This spreads out the responsibilities between the leader and the team and allows everyone to take ownership for the solution.

In this case, the executives began seeing how they were contributing to the problem. They weren't cultivating strategic thinking and planning through job responsibilities and incentive structure. They realized they weren't communicating the need for strategic thinking, or even explaining what they meant by strategy versus tactics. Once they understood all this, the leaders started taking responsibility for the lack of strategic thinking throughout their organizations. They were no longer complaining about the problem; they were owning it. That's when real change can happen.

Share Your Assumpts!

Turning your assumptions into Assumpts! is a powerful way to generate transformation. Sharing these Assumpts! with your group is a highly effective catalyst of change. This is why I suggested these business executives share what they learned with their teams to promote discussion and then action. Here is one way I suggested the business leaders frame those discussions.

Leveraging the Assumpt! to Promote Strategic Thinking

1. **Engage your teams:**
   a. Review the concept of the Assumpt!
   b. Provide permission to discuss content openly. See if the insights generated by you and your peers resonate with them.

2. **Motivate your group to "think differently":**
   a. Select up to three of the Assumpts! Have your group challenge them. For example, "I am too busy carrying out tactics and thus have no time to think strategically."
   b. Explore the reasons your group feels that way. Discuss what "strategy" means to them. Identify times when they can think "strategically.

3. **Compare your thinking:**
   a. Ask your group to share their Assumpts! as to why they think people prefer to think tactically versus strategically.
   b. Show and review the Assumpts! of other business leaders on this topic.
   c. Explore the discrepancies as well as similarities to find a common ground on which to discuss making some changes.

We All Do It

It's quite common to get frustrated with another person in your group for not thinking the same way as you do or to become angry when the person acts differently than you would have under the same conditions. Team members can spend an inordinate amount of time obsessing over why someone didn't "do it this way" rather than focusing their energy on collectively solving a shared problem.

For example, it's easy for you, as a team member, to feel that "I am the only one who cares" because you assume everyone must share the same enthusiasm you have for the project. This results in your taking on too much work that justifies your assumption but further alienates your team members. The sooner you recognize your assumption and turn it into an Assumpt!, the faster you will explore the reality of that Assumpt! and decide how you want to manage it.

People with synesthesia remind us that you can go through much of your life believing "everyone thinks like you." The key point is to understand that you have a natural tendency to see the world through your eyes, which can narrow your focus in building successful relationships and stimulating business growth. On the other hand, you can turn this assumption into an Assumpt! and challenge it. Doing so opens doors to building better relationships, generating alignment, and stimulating growth.

CHAPTER 10

"I Googled It"

The Information Age represents a movement toward a knowledge-based society in which it is easy to share, transmit, and search for data.

Yet having easy and quick access to all this information—information that is frequently free—leads us to assume it is more accurate than it really is. This results in making decisions and taking actions that are not always rational or in our best interest.

The Wrong Person Wins, and the Right Person Loses

There are many attributes to winning such as talent, perseverance, motivation, and luck. But sometimes, it rests entirely on your name.

In 1976, Robert E. Casey was elected state treasurer of Pennsylvania. Though a political unknown, he received the popular vote because people mistook him for Robert P. Casey, a seasoned politician whose family name represented a legacy in Pennsylvania like the Kennedys in Massachusetts and the Bushes in Texas. People didn't notice that the two Robert Caseys had two different middle initials.

Two years later in 1978, the seasoned Robert P. Casey ran for governor at the same time a Robert P. Casey, school teacher and ice cream vendor, ran for state legislature.

The famous Robert P. Casey lost his gubernatorial race while the unknown Casey won in a contested fourteen-person race for lieutenant governor. It's a safe guess that a majority of voters believed that Robert P. Casey was running for both offices. These split votes were not enough to carry the governor's seat but were enough to win the lieutenant governor's seat.

Almost ten years later, Robert P. Casey ran again as governor. But this time he preempted having his name "stolen" by creating "The Real Bob Casey for Governor Committee." And he won!

This humorous story illustrates how easy it is to assume that one person is the same as another based on just a name. I know that I have done it, and my Assumpt! is that you have done the same.

Before we explore why this happens, let's adjust the calendar and suppose that the elections just discussed are taking place now, so people have the ability and time to visit the candidates' websites. Would this make a difference in the elections' outcomes?

Not necessarily. Even when people are given information and facts that clearly outline differences between two people, their assumptions often override the data. Let's begin with a TV show and celebrity to illustrate this point.

Meet *The Housewives*

Around 2005, the US cable network Bravo tested a reality-show concept based on a behind-the-scenes glimpse into a Southern-California gated community and the lives of the wealthy—specifically, the wealthy housewives who married into wealth or created their own wealth through successful businesses.

Figure 8. Meet *The Real Housewives*. (BravoWatch.com)

The reality show was called *The Real Housewives of Orange County*. The format was twofold. These women would sit together and talk about life, family, their husbands, and whatever else was on their minds. This footage would intercut with personal footage of daily activities and one-on-one interviews of them talking about the other women. The show was a hit, and within a decade had become a franchise. There are *Real Housewives* shows in the United States about women in New York, New Jersey, and Miami while the international versions include housewives from France, Israel, Australia, and Brazil.

The host of the original series, and now executive producer, facilitated the conversation between the housewives, engaged them in confrontations, and often had to act as mediator when things got a bit heated—both verbally and sometimes physically.

The Other Andy Cohen

For those who are not familiar with the US *Housewives'* host and executive producer, I'll give you a little secret: His name is the same as mine. And, if you stretch things, you can find additional similarities between this Other Andy Cohen and me.

- We both grew up in the suburbs: he is from St. Louis, Missouri, and I am from Fair Lawn, New Jersey.

- Our mothers' first initials are the same: his mom is Evelyn, and mine is Estelle.

- We both wrote popular-selling books for the same publisher: St. Martin's Press.

- We both became known through our work in TV—his in reality programming and mine in writing, producing, and directing TV commercials.

- We are both paid to speak.

Still, we are more different than the same. The Other Andy Cohen is a social media maven with close to a million Facebook fans and over 1.5 million Twitter followers as of the time of this writing—in fact, he has sent close to fifty thousand personal tweets. My social media stats don't even come close. The Other Andy Cohen has been a TV host for twenty years. I appear on TV occasionally. He is gay. I am straight. And one look at these side-by-side pictures demonstrates further differences.

Figure 9. *Left,* The Other Andy Cohen; *right,* the author
(author photo by Howard Schatz)[1]

Still, this doesn't stop people from confusing us. It started years ago when I was interviewed on a business cable network in Mexico where the host asked me specific questions regarding dangerous assumptions of leadership in business. In other words, the context of the discussion was clear.

Yet when I received a video of the interview, the title superimposed under my picture on the screen translated roughly to "Andy Cohen, Executive Vice President of Development and Talent of the television cable network 'Bravo.'" (See Figure 10.)

Figure 10. Andy Cohen lost in translation (WOBI)

You might excuse this error to language differences. But then how do you explain when it happens on your own turf? I discovered that a company promoting keynote speakers had me listed as one of its clients. I didn't know what this company was, but its website clearly stated below my name, "Challenging Assumptions," a description I often use to explain what I talk about (Figure 11).

Yet when I looked at my picture, I saw the Other Andy Cohen instead.

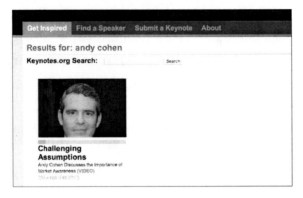

Figure 11. The Other Andy Cohen's face with my bio

As the Other Andy Cohen's popularity has grown, so have the number of his fans contacting me via phone calls, social media, and letters sent to my office. People send me a variety of things, including ideas for new *Housewives'* series, provocative pictures of themselves as they lobby to be on the show, products to try out, and even requests to pay their rent due to hardships. Once a marijuana distributor who wanted to brand Andy Cohen's name on a particular variety of weed solicited me. And if they don't want something from Andy Cohen, they have a complaint. Here are a few messages I've received:

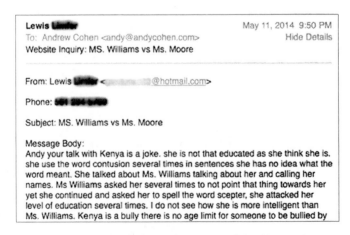

Figure 12. Complaining about one of the *Housewives*

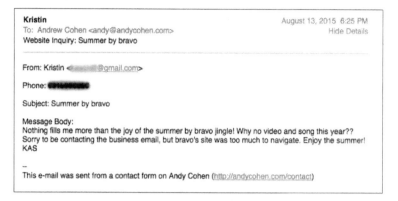

Figure 13. Idea for a new *Housewives* show

Figure 14. Suggestion for Bravo jingle

Desperately Seeking Andy Cohen

How do these people find me? What hurdles do they have to overcome to connect? I find it fascinating that most email contacts come through one of two websites: andycohenworldwide.com or andycohen.com.

And if you consider the steps these individuals take to write to me, it becomes even more interesting. The Other Andy Cohen's fans come to my home page, click on the navigational link that says "Contact," and then fill in a form requiring name, phone number, email address, and reason for contacting. Along the way, text, videos, and photos on my company website clearly show who I am and the services my firm and I provide. In other words, all the data is there to educate visitors to make the right decision in seeking out the Andy Cohen they are trying to reach. And yet people who want the Other Andy Cohen still contact me.

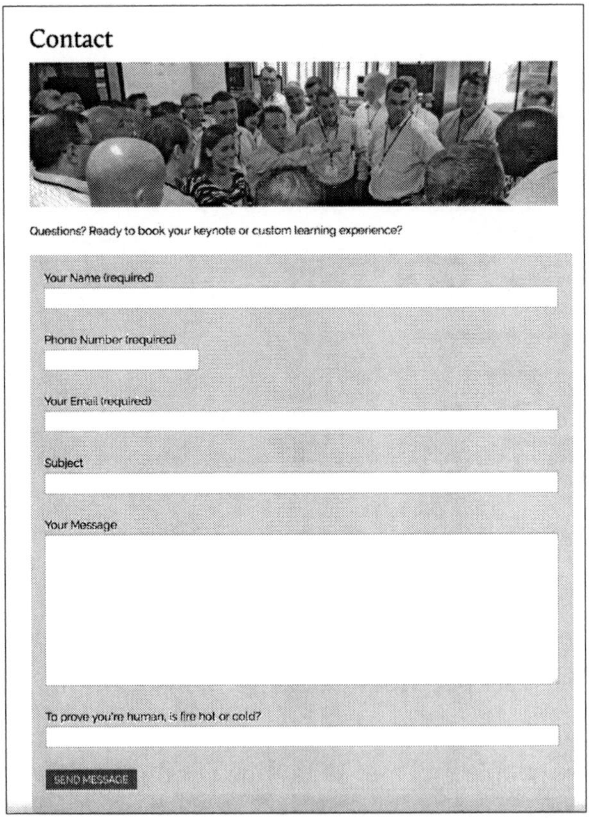

Figure 15. The author's "Contact" page that people use to reach out to the Other Andy Cohen

It's a gift to experience being a celebrity and having people reach out to you with overflowing praise, even if they are referring to someone else. Still, over the years I have wrestled with how to turn this unique experience of being able to see how much people care for, worship, and sometimes condemn a celebrity into a lesson about an assumption we all make. During this time, I have experimented with this story via keynotes and seminars. Watching people's reactions and then getting their personal feedback have been the impetus for including this story in the book. The story, while humorous, is also poignant. It's easy to judge others for following this specific assumption until we do it ourselves.

So, are these people who mistake me for the Other Andy Cohen stupid? Ignorant? Poor readers? Before we judge them too harshly, I would like to ask you a question that is biblical in nature and has to do with animals:

> What is the total number of each animal that Moses took on the ark with him during the Great Flood?

Please answer the question before you continue.

If you are like most people, you said, "two." But look at it one more time. In the popular Bible story, who took the animals on the ark? Moses? Or *Noah*? If you answered wrong, it's because you mistook one identity for another. This is called the *Moses illusion*, and it represents a behavior in which people associate certain words as similar when they are not. In this case, Moses and Noah share similar traits. They're both biblical characters; had beards; dealt with the seas; lived a long time ago; and are figures from our childhood.

So does the Moses illusion explain why people assume I am the Other Andy Cohen? Partially, due to the fact that people don't differentiate the name and thus attribute us as having similar traits.

The Google Illusion

But there is another factor I call the *Google illusion*. This term represents the assumption that if you Google it (or Bing it or Safari it), the information you come to is true. In other words, the act of searching is taken as providing authentication rather than the additional and necessary task of checking the quality of the information the search has supplied.

The Google illusion can take a number of forms:

"I Read It in the Papers"

Attributing credibility of information based on the media that delivers that information is nothing new. In 1898, publishers William Randolph Hearst and Joseph Pulitzer used sensation journalism to stoke the embers of the Spanish-American War with stories that were often made up just to create headlines that sold newspapers.

"I Heard It on the Radio"

In 1938, as many as a million people were convinced Earth was at war with Mars. Their source? Fictional news reports coming from the radio drama *War of the Worlds*, narrated by actor and soon-to-be filmmaker Orson Welles. These listeners had missed the opening introduction explaining the drama and assumed its reality because it was "heard on the radio."

"I Saw It on TV"

In the late 1950s, America met, for the first time, pitchman Ron Popeil on late-night TV. His commercials, which ran for decades, sold timesaving inventions that let you "slice and dice" food items with ease for the cost of just pennies. Initially, these products were sold direct on TV, but the real profit was generated through retail sales that were driven by a claim that added instant credibility to these products: "As Seen on TV."

"I Googled It"

Today, the Internet allows you to find the information you need quickly, easily, and without cost. Search engine technologies have changed our lives for the better. In an instant, we are connected to information that saves time, educates, entertains, and can even save lives.

But unlike other media, search engines are much more powerful because anyone with an Internet connection can access them for free. The point is that search engines bring you data but are theoretically agnostic regarding the data's quality. After all, it's just a search, though a highly sophisticated one. Still, over time, the phrase "I Googled it" has become an expression used to legitimize the quality of information. "How did you know?" is often followed by "I Googled it." This is a dangerous assumption because the act of searching is actually just that: a way to access what you are looking for. The responsibility for knowing whether that information is credible is ultimately up to you.

For example, have you ever been in a discussion about some piece of information and the other person pulls out a smartphone and searches for it? And in less than a minute, the person provides the answer? Problem solved, right?

But often it is not. Frequently, people grab the first piece of information that supports their viewpoint. Often, that source is Wikipedia, which is a great reference source but not always the gold standard. In 2005, *Businessweek* interviewed Jimmy Wales, founder of Wikipedia, and asked him, "Do you think students and researchers should cite Wikipedia?" He replied, "No, I don't think people should cite it, and I don't think people should cite Britannica, either . . . People shouldn't be citing encyclopedias in the first place. Wikipedia and other encyclopedias should . . . give good, solid background information to inform your studies for a deeper level."[2]

I agree with Jimmy Wales. In writing this book, Wikipedia was often my first research source. But it was more the beginning of the research than the end. Often, my Assumpt! was that Wikipedia provided enough depth, so I resisted spending the time doing extra research. Yet when I disciplined myself to go further, I discovered that the depth of information on a topic significantly increased.

What feeds into the "Google illusion" is *confirmation bias*. This psychological term refers to paying more attention to information that supports your beliefs while ignoring information that opposes them. For example, a smoker may seek out articles that downplay the dangers of cigarettes and ignore those articles that talk about their dangers. In other words, you ignore key information that presents a truer picture of things or their reality.

My Assumpt! is this bias explains an underlying reason why once people find contact information with the name Andy Cohen, they ignore the data that tells them I am not the Andy Cohen they are looking for. But the Google illusion amplifies this bias on a grand scale as we become more and more dependent on search engines to provide us the information we are looking for, allowing this bias to kick in.

It's important to note that when you search for "Andy Cohen," it is the Other Andy Cohen who dominates (to my frustration) the search page. So I am not sure how people looking for him find me. And neither do they. Here are a few of their responses when I reached out to them to find out how they got to my website:

- "Andy so sorry—found this (your contact info) on Google."

- "You were the first thing that came up in my search."

- "I just found you."

The research I have conducted is small in number and not conclusive. But the Google illusion is a reminder of both how easily we latch onto search information once we think we found what we are looking for and how we assume that information is correct.

Crisis Equals Danger and Opportunity, True or Not

Here is an example of how the Google illusion affected me. Chances are you have heard someone say that the word *crisis* is composed of two different symbols in Chinese—one means danger, the other opportunity. It's a terrific concept that allows us to approach each difficult situation with an open mind. John F. Kennedy cited the story during a speech in 1959,[3] and in 2007, Al Gore used it in a Nobel lecture[4] and Condoleezza Rice in a Middle East peace talk.[5] The idea has become widely known.

I was introduced to this concept after working with an insurance group in Asia. One day, one of the participants, who was Chinese, gave me a hand-drawn scroll painted by her father. The two symbols drawn created the word *crisis*.

Figure 16. Scroll with the Chinese word for "crisis"
(author's personal collection)

I was baffled. My session was focused on giving the group a way to embrace change by challenging their assumptions—a key process for thinking differently and making better decisions. My initial concern was that I had missed the mark and failed in getting the message heard or understood.

Then, the participant explained that *crisis* is made up of two words: danger and opportunity. She further explained that my session uncovered the danger in treating our assumptions as truths rather than beliefs. It also showed the opportunity in leveraging your assumptions to open new doors that did not exist before, to uncover the ideas hidden right in front of you, and to discover ways to change.

That scroll hangs on the wall in my office. It reminds me that no matter how you see the world, there is always another perspective that can be of equal or greater value. Even in crisis, there is hope and opportunity.

I loved this story and assumed that based on the participant's Chinese heritage, it was true, so I soon began to incorporate it into my lectures.

That's when I decided to learn more about the story since I was talking about something told to me but never truly researched. So I Googled it.

And when I did, I came across close to 200 million searches, and glancing at the top three all supported its meaning, so I assumed the concept was true. I was subject to the Google illusion. But then I decided to turn that assumption into an Assumpt! and challenge it. So I scrolled further, and around the fifth search, I began to discover that the saying might not translate as closely as many suggested it did.

The first symbol of the word, wēi, definitely means "danger." But the second symbol, jī, can mean anything from "airplane" to "secret," depending on the context. Thus is the nature of Mandarin Chinese.

I had to dig deep to question the authenticity of this saying. And the more I dug, the more conflicting information appeared.

I still like what the concept represents. But since I can't find a definitive answer, I have stopped using this metaphor as an example in my lectures.

Tools: Seeing the Differences When Differences Matter

We live in a wonderful and amazing time in which online access to information makes you smarter, helps you manage your life better, and provides you the answers you seek. Yet the ease and speed of acquiring that information also feed into a number of behaviors that lead us to assume the first pieces of information supporting our beliefs represent the truth that we seek. The Moses illusion leads you to treat similarities as the same. Confirmation bias tends to let you select the information that supports your beliefs while ignoring contrary information that may be closer to the reality. This feeds into the Google illusion that confuses the act of searching with the accuracy of the information sought.

Next time you or someone else says, "I Googled it," think about the conditions that led to the search to see what assumptions might have been generated. Here are some strategies that might help:

- **The more you want something, such as connecting with the Other Andy Cohen, the greater the tendency to look for the similarities and ignore the cues and data that suggest conflicts.** So instead of immediately investing in those similarities, reject them. This will help you identify the differences a lot faster.

- **Constantly ask yourself, "What conclusions am I drawing based on limited information?"** For example, search for "Jonathan West oil business," and you will see that he is indeed in that business. It would then be natural to assume that he has a certain level of wealth, not bothering to find out that he is in the less lucrative business of selling *olive* oil.

- **The old carpenter's rule to "measure twice and cut once" reminds you to double-check your information before you invest in it.** Turn the assumption that the first search results that pop up are the most relevant into an Assumpt! Then, dig a bit deeper. It will take more time, but that's the cost of accuracy when it matters most.

CHAPTER 11

The Experts Say It Can't Be Done

How strongly do you believe in yourself? Are you willing to confront and challenge the multiple times the assumption "it can't be done" crosses your path in life? This chapter shares the story of a young entrepreneur who comes to Manhattan with just a vision. He opens his first store in such a competitive area that even his real estate agent doesn't want to give him a lease for fear his store will not survive. Then, his business partner fears the store will go under after a competitor lowers its prices. Yet this entrepreneur not only succeeds but also thrives, creating a whole new retail segment.

Behind the Scenes: Breakfast with Solomon Choi

16 Handles had been open just two weeks when I first stepped through its doors. The lines pouring into the street drew me in, and within seconds, I was part of the enthusiastic crowd bubbling with excitement over this new experience. Within a week, I reached out to Solomon Choi, 16 Handles's founder, requesting an interview. At the time, Choi was a struggling entrepreneur, so my Assumpt! is that his motivation to meet might have been driven as much by the free breakfast as the opportunity to talk about business. Over the next five years, we would get together again so I could update my notes and share in his progress.[1] I would also send my NYU marketing students there as a homework assignment about empowering the customer.

In 2008, Solomon Choi arrived in New York City with a vision that within just a few years, he would alter the retail landscape of Manhattan and beyond. Choi is the founder of 16 Handles, the first self-serve frozen yogurt (fro-yo) retail store in the NYC metropolitan area.

He opened his first store a year later and over time has spawned a number of 16 Handles shops along with dozens of competitors who have copied his concept. You can recognize a 16 Handles shop as many of them feature floor-to-ceiling glass walls that invite you into Day-Glo orange-and-green environments filled with colorful booths and cushioned seats, digital displays showing Snapchats of customers eating, and sixteen self-serve machines delivering a variety of fun flavors like American Apple Pie, Caramel Popcorn Finale, Graham Cracker, and Euro Tart. Many of the competitors try to mimic this look and the flavors. Most don't survive. 16 Handles, however, keeps thriving.

"It's a Bad Business Idea"

Choi moved to New York from Los Angeles and roomed in a tiny East Village apartment converted from a one bedroom into four bedrooms with one shared bathroom. The only thing he brought with him was a few years of experience working in his father's restaurant that catered to an all-you-can-eat sushi crowd and the time he spent working in a small candy shop that dabbled in self-serve yogurt. These two very different jobs served as the building blocks for a concept that would translate to delivering a unique customer experience.

Figure 17. Solomon Choi (*center*), founder of 16 Handles, at his flagship store
(photo courtesy of Solomon Choi)

But this concept had many naysayers even before it got off the
ground. Choi's cousin was working in finance, and Choi's social circle
was primarily other investment bankers who graduated from top-
notch universities. When Choi shared his vision with these bankers,
the majority rejected the concept and said, "it can't be done," citing
what they had learned in business school:

- The cost to buy the fro-yo from the distributor was low and
  readily available, which meant that anyone could do this.

- The price of entry against the competition of other established
  yogurt and ice cream brands was too high. In other words, in
  order to compete, 16 Handles would have to invest significant
  dollars in marketing and promotions to draw customers away
  from these big brands.

- The original store had limited seating, which meant customers couldn't hang around.

- The business would die during winter.

Choi, however, politely ignored what the bankers learned in school and business because he was armed with something more powerful: a vision for creating an eating experience that would leave people standing out on the street to get in. And this is exactly what happened within the first months of opening his store.

The idea of offering people control of serving themselves a fun and healthy food in an equally fun and healthy environment is a powerful combination that New Yorkers had yet to experience.

"Too Much Competition"

At first, Choi struggled to find a suitable location to open his frozen yogurt shop. He spent his days walking from the Financial District to Times Square, looking for potential storefronts. He resisted engaging a real estate agent, mostly because he assumed an agent would put him in a space as quickly as possible with an eye toward a commission and not on the suitability of the location.

Choi quickly realized, however, that walking up and down the streets of a strange new city was not a great way to find real estate, so he begrudgingly found a real estate agent. The agent showed Choi various areas of the city that would make sense, warning him to stay out of the East Village, an area saturated with frozen treat stores. But Choi gravitated toward the East Village, mostly because he realized the foot traffic in the area was mostly women ages eighteen to thirty-four—his target demographic.

Choi found an open space in the East Village that was already perfectly suited to a frozen yogurt store. But the real estate agent warned him against it. Why? The space was the former home of a Cold Stone Creamery, which had gone out of business in just five months because of the intense competition in the area. Ben & Jerry's, Pinkberry, Red Mango, and Tasti D-Lite were just yards away from the storefront.

The agent begged Choi to go elsewhere. The message was clear: Opening a successful store in the middle of such fierce competition? It can't be done.

Choi later learned that the agent was merely trying to dissuade him because commercial real estate agents don't always receive full commission unless a store stays open for a year or more. It was safer for the agent to push Choi into an area with less competition. But Choi was persistent: If his target customers were already in the area buying frozen yogurt, why go anywhere else?

Choi made an Assumpt! and challenged it. Instead of seeing a "wall" of competitors, he saw a "door" for opportunity. Choi knew his success lay in creating an experience that would separate him from the competition. Therefore, he strove to create a lifestyle experience based around fun and creativity in making your own dessert. He saw the space from the viewpoint of his potential customers, who wanted a destination that offered a healthier alternative to ice cream and fostered creativity and uniqueness. He wasn't afraid of the competition. In his mind, the competition should be afraid of him. And he was right.

Within the first year, three of the brand-name competitors in the area were gone. And even with limited seating, crowds of people continued to line up outside 16 Handles to create their own sweet desserts, and they stayed until midnight or later, adding to the fun-filled atmosphere.

"We're Too Expensive"

Then one day a seeming disaster struck. Choi's cousin, who had become his business partner, approached him with the depressing news that a fro-yo company around the corner was offering a similar product for ten cents less an ounce. According to Choi, a brief conversation ensued. "This will put us out of business," his cousin lamented. Instead, Choi responded, "This will make us even more successful."

Solomon Choi knew that the success of 16 Handles was based on the client's unique experience. Those who tried the competitor at a lesser price would realize that going to 16 Handles is as much about the atmosphere as it is about the cost of the product. And once they discovered that the competitor couldn't replicate the 16 Handles experience, they would be back. He was right. Within a year, the other business folded as 16 Handles thrived.

I have travelled the country observing a variety of companies that offer frozen yogurt dispensaries but lack a vibrant customer experience. They too often fold without understanding why.

16 Handles survived and thrived because Choi refused to take "it can't be done" for an answer. To date of this writing, 16 Handles has forty-two stores in six states and two countries.

How 16 Handles Thought Differently

Seating

The flagship store offered two small tables and an outside bench, enough only to seat about a dozen people. This turned out to be an advantage for the store, however, as people flooded out onto the street devouring the fro-yo in their Day-Glo cups with their Day-Glo spoons and thus advertising the product and experience. In addition, the limited size of the restaurant resulted in lines outside the door. You could actually see people who had been to the store before explaining to others how the process of self-serve worked and the others' excitement and anticipation for trying out the experience for the first time. The key to remember is that sometimes you can turn a negative situation that appears to be a barrier (limited seating) into an opportunity. What limitations do you face that might work in your favor?

Holding Your Price

It's a common retail strategy when a competitor enters the field to have a sale or to lower your price for a period of time to discourage people from leaving your store. But 16 Handles chose not to compete on price but on making the store a destination that was fun (as the stores have expanded, so has the seating to include modern space-age décor with wide booths and small tables and chairs to form your own seating— and of course there's the stores' famous Day-Glo green, orange, and muted red), environmentally friendly (Choi originally launched the store with wooden spoons as opposed to plastic), healthy (gluten-free, kosher, low fat, vegan), and socially connected (it was one of the first food retailers to publicly display live tweets and Facebook posts in the store). The point is that customers are price sensitive, but they don't buy only on price. 16 Handles isn't the cheapest fro-yo store, but it strives to make sure it's seen as a good value. What is the value that you bring to the job or offer your customer that goes beyond price?

Size Doesn't Always Matter

When 16 Handles first opened, there were three brand-name, established competitors—Red Mango, Pinkberry, and Ben & Jerry's— within a two-block radius. There were also a handful of smaller ice cream and frozen yogurt stores in the same radius. Yet none of these stores offered the same type of experience as 16 Handles. Within two years, Red Mango and Ben & Jerry's were gone as well as many of the local vendors. Additional self-serve fro-yo establishments have since opened and quickly closed as none of these stores could capture the same experience as 16 Handles, even though their flavors and candy bar toppings were similar or the same. It's important to note that in an age of popular brands that monopolize their business categories—for example, Google, Uber, Whole Foods—there are still opportunities to create niche businesses by offering a unique service that customers cannot find elsewhere. The success of Trader Joe's is one example.

Trader Joe's migrated from a chain of convenience stores in the 1950s to specialty-food stores in the late 1960s, packaging, as its website states, "innovative, hard-to-find, great-tasting foods,"[2] which allowed the store to keep the cost down. The classic example is the "Two-Buck Chuck," which was its famous offering of a private-label bottle of wine for just $2 (now $3). There is nothing fancy about the décor, all the display signs are handwritten, and the workers seem happy to be there.

What 16 Handles and Trader Joe's teach us is that regardless of price, the overall customer experience is what provides a competitive edge over existing, larger brands and what sustains a business over time. So if you assume that price is your competitive edge, turn that into an Assumpt! and challenge it to discover what other attributes your customers will flock to and perceive as value.

CHAPTER 12

Please Fasten Your Seat Belts

Getting people's attention takes work. But once you have them listening, how well prepared are you to make sure they understand what is being said so that they can comply with the rules? This chapter explores a global situation in which an important announcement is typically ignored, even though the information is designed to save your life.

We are, of course, talking about the pre-flight safety announcement. The assumption that people are naturally apathetic to this announcement, especially when asked to follow rules, is just part of the story. The other part examines the responsibility (or lack thereof) of the leadership who are tasked to set and enforce the rules to comply and suggests that perhaps there is a better way not only to ask people for their attention but also to help them understand and retain this vital information.

From Nurse to Hostess to Taskmaster

In the 1930s, all airline stewardesses, referred to as "sky girls," had to be registered nurses. Why? Well, in addition to their jobs of serving meals and sometimes even fueling the plane, the federal airline administration wanted people on board capable of dealing with medical emergencies. During World War II, these nurses were recruited to serve in the armed forces, and the requirement for stewardesses to also be nurses was dropped—in large part because there simply weren't enough nurses available.

In less than two decades, these sky girls were transformed into employees who couldn't be married or pregnant, wore miniskirts, and seductively said things in commercials like, "come fly with me." They were still trained in safety, but the greater emphasis was on honing their skills as waitresses and hostesses whose purpose was to assure that you had the most "delicious" and "comfortable" flight.

The Civil Rights Act of 1964 opened the job up to males as well, and the term *stewardess* became *flight attendant.*

Today, the role of the flight attendant has morphed into a multitasking taskmaster who works to get you to your seat; stows your luggage—either above your head or underneath your seat; delivers your food; and picks up your garbage at the end of the flight.

The glamour days of flying are over, and even those who travel in first class complain about the inconsistent quality of service.

It's sad that as passengers seek the cheapest flight and airlines seek to cut costs, the true value of flight attendants has been diminished. What is lost is that their main purpose is to help get you safely from Point A to Point B and to be prepared if there is an incident.

This brings us back to the pre-flight safety announcement (PFSA). The PFSA's purpose is to provide the passenger the rules of flight (e.g., buckle your seat belt during takeoff) and more importantly the rules of engagement during an emergency (e.g., if you are travelling with a child, put your oxygen mask on first). The expected outcome of the PFSA is that you are properly prepared to deal with an unexpected situation during the flight.

The International Civil Aviation Organization (ICAO), a special agency of the United Nations, issues the overall rules, and each country has its own aviation administration to interpret and oversee them.

Here is what the US Federal Aviation Administration (FAA) provided as the reason for the PFSA. The document is from 2003 (the latest version I could find) and states:

> **BACKGROUND.** An alert, knowledgeable person has a much better chance of surviving any life- or injury-threatening situation that could occur during passenger-carrying operations in civil aviation. Therefore, the Federal Aviation Administration (FAA) requires a passenger information system for US air carriers and commercial operators that includes both oral briefings and briefing cards. Every airline passenger should be motivated to focus on the safety information in the passenger briefing; however, motivating people, even when their own personal safety is involved, is not easy. One way to increase passenger motivation is to make the safety information briefings and cards as interesting and attractive as possible.

The FAA went on to say that it "encourages individual operators to be innovative in their approach in imparting such information."[1]

What irks me is not that most passengers and people who work at airlines acknowledge the challenges of engagement. It's that the airlines persist in repeating the same PFSA process thousands of times a day around the globe, millions of times a year, knowing that few are truly paying attention or can follow the rules in case of an emergency. Relatively the same message is delivered on a plane taking off in Bangkok, Thailand, and in Bangor, Maine, and in all cases, barely anyone is paying attention.

The PFSA is designed to save your life, not bore you to death. In the '60s, '70s, and '80s, as the laundry list of PFSA items grew from no smoking in the lavatory to please turn off all portable electronic devices (PEDs) before taking off, so did the apathy toward delivering and receiving the announcement.

Have you ever noticed that when one person in a group yawns, you start to feel that way too? Yawning is contagious. Well, it is no different here. As the flight attendants were commanded to deliver a message that was lengthy and that no one listened to, they became bored giving it. Passengers picked up on that, and even fewer listened, so the situation got worse and worse.

Humor Takes Off

Then, in the late 2000s, a few attendants began a small revolt. With the approval of their airline and the FAA, they began taking charge and finding new and fun ways to deliver the PFSA in an attempt to gain passengers' interest (i.e., get them to pay attention).

In 2009, for example, flight attendant David Holmes delivered the PFSA in rap. This is what Holmes told his passengers on a Southwest flight before he helped change the PFSA forever: "I've had five flights today, and I can't do the regular boring announcement again; otherwise, I am going to put myself to sleep," Then, he began to rap. Here is some of what he sang:

> Shortly after takeoff, first things first,
> There's soft drinks and coffee to quench your thirst. . . .
> Carry-on items go under the seat
> In front of you so none of you have things by your feet.
> If you have a seat on a row with an exit,
> We're gonna talk to you, so you might as well expect it.

You gotta help evacuate in case we need you.
If you don't want to, then we're gonna reseat you.

Holmes's rap was met with cheers and applause and was recorded and posted on YouTube, receiving over 1.2 million visits so far.[2] Other flight attendants followed with their own unique spins on the PFSA. One very clever attendant, again from Southwest, said the following, which landed her on *The Ellen DeGeneres Show*:

> Right on top is a safety information card. Take it out, check it out; you'll notice in the highly unlikely event that the captain lands us near a hot tub, everybody gets their very own teeny-weeny yellow Southwest bikini. One size fits all . . .

As she is saying this, another attendant is showing people the yellow vests. This video has received over twenty-two million visits, and you can hear the passengers laughing along with the announcement.[3]

These flight attendants deserve our applause for taking on the responsibility of engaging passengers. They help set in motion attempts by other airlines to deliver the PFSA in clever ways via video.

One of the pioneers in using video was Air New Zealand who had the captain and the crew deliver the PFSA in the nude. These real employees had their bodies spray-painted and were then cleverly positioned within the plane to hide the more risqué body parts as they delivered the safety measure. In 2012, Air New Zealand employees dressed as characters from *The Hobbit* as they gave the announcement. The video even included a cameo by Sir Peter Jackson, the director of *The Hobbit* trilogy filmed in New Zealand.[4] The dialogue is brilliant as it mimics the tone of the movie while delivering the key information.

Over time, all the major airlines have experimented with clever and creative executions that engage passengers. Virgin Atlantic uses cartoons while Virgin America uses contemporary song and dance. Turkey's Pegasus Airlines uses Marvel Comics superheroes.

Whenever I travel, I watch people watching PFSA videos (I know, I know—I should be watching the video, too). Over time, I have seen more and more people listening as well as laughing. Once in a while at a party, I even hear people talk about these videos.

No Laughing Matter

Unfortunately, engagement doesn't equal retention. How often do you remember TV commercials for their humor or graphics yet cannot recall the name of the product, brand, or, more importantly, the details of the message? Data from Nielsen, a research company measuring viewer behavior, reported in 2010 that the general recall of TV ads was 46 percent but message recall was 21 percent.[5]

The limited research that has been done into the effectiveness of the more entertaining pre-flight safety announcements shows the same thing is going on.

In a 2015 published study, Dr. Brett Molesworth and Dimuth Seneviratne from the University of New South Wales in Australia found that the use of humor or a celebrity in delivering the PFSA can boost recall as much as 15 percent.[6]

The same research, however, shows that the level of recall, even with humorous videos, is normally below a 50 percent threshold. And after two hours, there is a drop in the retention rate. This is a disturbing statistic, given that many flights last far longer than 120 minutes.[7]

Another way to measure engagement is to explore a passenger's ability to pay attention. Mr. Dimuth Seneviratne, a member of Dr. Molesworth's research team, conducted a study into the effectiveness of these briefings in maintaining the attention of passengers. The number of times individuals looked away from watching the video was examined as well as information they recalled. Again, the humorous briefing proved to be the most effective. Participants looked away on average only one time when humor featured in the video. When the video was void of humor or a celebrity, individuals looked away on average three times as much. Participants in the humor group also recalled more key safety messages than any other group; however, recall was also below the 50 percent threshold as mentioned before.[8]

In a study published in the 2011 *Journal of Marketing Communications*, Volume 17, Issue 5, Dr. Fong Yee Chan reported that humor enhances engagement but may disrupt the processing of key information.[9]

Additional research is needed, especially in light of the ever-evolving use of humor and other engaging executions in PFSA videos. But my Assumpt! is that improving PFSA retention via humorous and creative video executions is not a substitute for improving the overall PFSA effectiveness and is distracting us from a bigger issue. Here's why.

People who create advertising are trained in finding creative ways to use media to sell products. In a media like TV, the goal is to communicate one or two key points—such as "this product cleans faster" or "this service will help your kids become smarter." Yet, as mentioned before, only one-fifth of the time does someone actually recall a specific message—and that is when only one or two points are being made.

PFSAs are designed to communicate 13–16 important points—in less than three minutes. Imagine if you just joined a company and were asked to watch a three-minute video covering thirteen actions. How much could you actually retain? Especially if you knew no one would test you later? To emphasize this point, here is a highly abbreviated, paraphrased checklist containing information points set by the ICAO,

FAA, and other national civil-aviation authorities. Please note, not all countries require the same pieces of information. For example, the United States and some other countries do not require demonstrating the brace position. But even with certain exceptions by individual countries, this partial list demonstrates the breadth of information needed to be absorbed in a short period of time:

- Demonstrate the use of seat belts during takeoff and landing and during turbulence.
- Explain the no-smoking rules in the plane and lavatory.
- Make reference to reviewing the safety card in the seat pocket.
- Explain emergency exits and how people should deplane in case of emergency.
- Discuss the use of oxygen masks.
- Present the location and use of life vests, rafts, and flotation devices.
- Demonstrate the brace position.
- Remind flyers of the position of seat backs and tray tables during takeoff and flight.

My Assumpt! is that most people would agree that passengers feel little consequence in not paying attention. This is, in part, driven by apathy and the fact that getting to the airport is actually more dangerous than flying on the plane. The odds of being on a plane that crashes are one in ten million for the top thirty-nine airlines with the best accident records and one in 1.5 million for the bottom thirty-nine with the worst accident records.[10] Overconfidence also plays a role in that most passengers assume they know the drill, even though when the real test comes, they often fail. Just take a look at pictures of the people standing on the wing of US Airways Flight 1549 that crash-landed on the Hudson River in 2009. It appears that less than three-quarters put on their life vests.

Another powerful reason people don't pay attention is because they've been desensitized by a ritual that rarely changes. The PFSA is given at roughly the same time before takeoff, it covers basically the same 13–16 points of information, and it's either delivered via video or personal announcement. In other words, the PFSA experience rarely varies. In fairness to the airlines, they are trying to rotate PFSA videos to address this issue.

While the passenger must assume responsibility for paying attention to the PFSA, it is ultimately the responsibility of the people who set and deliver the rules to make sure the messages are listened to and internalized.

But as long as the PFSA is treated as a boring message to get through, this will not happen. The Federal Aviation Administration sets the rules for what needs to be covered during a flight. It doesn't matter if the PFSA is engaging or not; as long as the airline communicates the rules, it is legally covered. There are no penalties for passenger lack of understanding or compliance—well, none immediately. Dr. Brett Molesworth suggests that in the future this could become an issue if the aircraft crashes and the passengers do not behave as they should have based on the information in these boring briefings.[11]

An "A" for Retention

Now, imagine if the FAA was responsible for making sure people retained the information. Think of what would happen to the PFSA if airlines were graded on how many points passengers could actually recall? My Assumpt! is that this would change the entire PFSA experience.

Before you dismiss this idea by assuming it is an unrealistic goal and there are no ways you can measure the PFSA's influence on every passenger, consider this.

Imagine taking your test for your driver's license without actually having driven a car before. Just before the test, you are given a three-minute video with thirteen key points about the safety of driving, which you must employ while in the car. Sounds silly, right? Driving is learned primarily through experience, in which you ride and control the car. During the learning process, you also have the opportunity to interact with other drivers, ask questions, and attend classes that teach and test you on the rules of the road. In other words, learning is an experience obtained over time with trial and error through interaction.

The goal of the PFSA should be like learning the rules of the road and how to act when on the road (or in a crash). Dependency on a three-minute video to deliver that goal isn't realistic. The way the airlines communicate the PFSA needs to be changed.

The way to make that change happen is to stop repeating the same ineffective behavior and discard the present process for something more effective. Figuring out what can be done is one of the exercises we conduct in my leadership workshops.

Think Outside the Video

In one workshop with senior executives, I ask them to take the role of the FAA and airline executives. They are told they will be responsible for making sure that people pay attention and internalize the various safety checkpoints.

Furthermore, I encourage them to think outside the video and focus beyond making the video or announcement more creative and to consider the overall passenger experience. Once you no longer restrict yourself on the present PFSA format, brilliant ideas begin to percolate. Here are a few of them:

- **Family Days:** Every airport invites parents, kids, and others to come onboard a real jet. When passengers take a seat, they are given a longer-version PFSA that allows them to ask questions and try out the equipment. The captain speaks to them about the importance of the PFSA and the key things to listen for. Having children learn the key points at an early age is an effective way to help them retain the info for every flight.

- **Airport Demonstration Sites:** Every airport has a demo site in the terminal where people can test out the equipment or actually test themselves on what to do during an emergency. I have never had to actually take out my flotation device and am not sure I could do it correctly if I actually had to.

- **Virtual Reality:** Captains learn to fly planes in part using virtual-reality tools that simulate flights. Why can't passengers go through a virtual experience that tests their ability to respond properly during a flight emergency?

- **Disaster Videos:** Once after takeoff, I watched an attendant ask a seasoned traveler a question about extracting the flotation device. The passenger didn't answer correctly. She then reminded him to pay attention next time.

    When I congratulated her on helping a passenger understand the importance of listening to the PFSA, she shared an interesting story. Her airline makes all the attendees watch a video of airline disasters. This was such a powerful experience for her that she had her kids watch it, and to this day, her kids make sure they know the proper exits on the plane before taking off and listen to the rules. Admittedly, some passengers would be too scared to watch a video like this. But my Assumpt! is that most of us can—and should—because once you see it, then you understand the reality of the PFSA's value. The FAA would be wise to make these films available to everyone who flies.

- **Video Gaming:** The availability of interactive monitors on the seat back in front of you is becoming standard. Why not turn the PFSA into a video game that you must participate in before you use the monitor? It would ask you multiple-choice questions for you to answer in a fun manner.

- **Online Messages:** Research shows that retention increases when you combine TV advertising with online banner ads.[12] Why not randomly rotate key safety-announcement messages when people are checking in online?

- **Explain Why:** George Hobica, renowned travel writer and founder of the online advisory airfarewatchdog.com, shared his experience after attending the British Airways Flight Safety Awareness Course that all flight crews go through. He said it really helped him appreciate the value of the PFSA. "You understand why some of those more obscure procedures and safety warnings are part of the flight experience," said Hobica. "I left the course thinking that more passengers would listen to the pre-flight safety demo if airlines shared some of this insider information before each flight, maybe mixing it up from time to time so that the demo doesn't get overly long and cause more people to tune out," he added.[13]

Hobica provided a number of examples that make the rules more understandable and relevant. He reported:

> Why do airlines dim the cabin lights during nighttime takeoffs and landings? You guessed it:

to help adjust your eyes to the dark (either inside a smoke-filled cabin or on a darkened runway). And why do some airlines ask that you keep your shoes on (except high heels, which can tear the slide) when taking off and landing? Because [in the case of a sudden evacuation] the runway might be burning hot after you jump down the slide.[14]

The ideas above are just a few of the innovative ones that were generated by challenging the Assumpt! that the PFSA is just that: an announcement. By taking the PFSA out of its normal framework, you now have the freedom to explore new ways to deliver key safety messages.

Applying Lessons of the PFSA to Your Business

If you can make the PFSA something people internalize and retain (and I believe you can), think about the ways you can communicate all the processes and procedures you need to get across to your employees or teams.

How many people actually read a new employee manual? When a new corporate strategy is launched, how many employees actually understand its key points (versus just repeating them) in a way that creates alignment between senior leadership and the rest of the company? When financial service companies, for example, are asked to comply with a growing number of regulations, do they really comprehend the rules, or do they just become a growing list of things to check off?

There are multiple lessons to learn from the present state of the PFSA, including what you need to focus on if you truly want people to pay attention and comply. It means identifying a number of assumptions and turning them into Assumpts! to challenge. Lessons include:

- **Responsibility:** What happens when you make the people responsible for setting the rules also responsible for making sure they are retained? Many readers will probably react and assume this isn't practical. For example, how can lawmakers be responsible for the outcome? But, on the other hand, if the laws are written in a way that people can't understand, who is responsible for that?

- **Understanding Why:** How well do your employees understand the reasons they are asked to do something? Businesses often assume that if they lay the rules out clearly, then people can follow. But understanding why something is the way it is makes it more relevant, and the more relevant the information, the easier it is to understand and the greater the motivation to comply.

- **Before You Add a New Rule:** Organizations assume that when there is a new rule, they can just add it to the existing list. Over time, however, the list becomes overwhelming to comprehend (as well as outdated). Perhaps it would be prudent to agree to eliminate one rule for every new rule added.

- **Repetition:** Houdini, one of the greatest escape artists ever, could swallow a key to regurgitate when needed to unlock handcuffs. He overcame the gag reflex by practicing key swallowing. What procedures does your business do on a regular basis that over time have desensitized people from listening to or engaging in them? Why not rotate the way messages are delivered through the organization instead of using the same format each time?

- **Cost:** I asked a few airline experts why the FAA or the airlines don't invest in overhauling the PFSA so that people retain the information rather than ignore it. Their answer? Airline improvements are driven by costs and potential profits. Improving the PFSA doesn't increase profits, and changing the process significantly is not where the airlines want to put their dollars.

  This is also why many organizations continue to employ the same ineffective means of communication that drive compliance. They assume that the cost to do things differently isn't justified. Keeping this assumption unchecked is why compliance often doesn't take off.

In Conclusion

You might be wondering why I am expressing a concern about the ineffectual PFSA when it's clear that the FAA, airlines, and even the passengers don't consider this an issue. The answer is simple: safety.

As I write this, I am listening to the news of a JetBlue flight diverted because of unexpected turbulence. Twenty-two passengers and two crew members were taken to the hospital for injuries sustained when the plane quickly lost altitude. A follow-up news article reported what passenger Christopher De Vries observed about his young daughters complying with the rules: that "he's glad he's been a 'stickler' for reminding them to fasten their seatbelts." Said De Vries: "They would have flown out of their seats had they not been strapped in."[15] It's easy to dismiss this as an isolated instance until it happens to you.

In other words, flight safety is relevant to everyone. If we are going to go through the motions to reflect this, let's find a way to make the words meaningful to everyone in a way that makes a difference. The assumption that this is a "communications" issue needs to be challenged. Complying with the PFSA and the millions of other messages designed to protect our safety and livelihood (like safe drinking water) is a leadership issue.

Keeping this assumption unchecked is why compliance in the marketplace often doesn't take off.

CHAPTER 13

Build It, and They Will Come

My Assumpt! is that you and I are not that different when it comes to daydreaming about having a great idea that everyone will love and that will make us millions. Deep down inside, we believe that if we could just build this product or this service, everyone would flock to us. The assumption that great ideas are like light beacons that draw people to you like magnets can prove to be quite dangerous, however. This chapter explores what happens when you act on this assumption and what is needed to challenge it.

Turning Your "Field of Dreams" into a Reality

In 1997, the early days of the Internet, I asked a senior executive why people would come to a website he was proposing to build. He answered without hesitation, saying, "If we build it, they will come."

Not only was he incorrect in assuming that people would flock to the company site as soon as it was built, he was also incorrect in the words he chose.

The actual saying is, "If you build it, he will come." The "you" refers to Kevin Costner who in the Oscar-winning movie *Field of Dreams* hears an internal voice speaking to him to mow down his cornfield and put up a baseball field. The "he will come" refers to Shoeless Joe

Jackson and other dead baseball players who will come and play once the baseball diamond and outfield is created.[1]

The movie was released in 1989, and a few years later, the phrase morphed, and the idea that "if you build something great, others will follow" caught on in the corridors of business. The dot-com start-ups were extremely vulnerable to this assumption only to discover that having a great idea is just part of the equation—cash flow, the ability to execute, smart marketing, etc. all contribute to the success of any innovative thinking.

But They Didn't Come

Large, successful global brands also succumb to the business mantra "build it, and they will come." Here are two examples.

When Home Depot launched its do-it-yourself (DIY) store in China, it bombed as most people in China don't like to do it themselves and, as a result, didn't come to the Home Depot stores. Walmart lost $1 billion when it was forced to pull out of Germany because of customers who never came due to differing cultural consumer and business practices.[2] Germans are less price-sensitive than Americans, weren't interested in having a store open for twenty-four hours, and utilized a distribution system favoring small- and medium-sized businesses.

American brands aren't the only ones who have suffered from the assumption that a brand that attracts loyalty in one country will do the same in another. I worked with one of Germany's leading appliance manufacturers who was seeking help in understanding why the US market wasn't falling head over heels with its products in the States. After all, the manufacturer was number one in its country.

In Chapter 9, we explored challenging the dangerous assumption that "the world thinks just like me," an assumption that feeds into making people and organizations assume that everyone thinks the same way—that transplanting success from one country to the next is a no-brainer. Overconfidence in your brand strength also leads to the assumption that people will be attracted to your product or service forever.

They Want to Come but Can't

But what if you are a well-recognized brand that wants to build something truly big and important only to realize there are no roads in which people could come, even if they want to?

This is the story of a small group of executives who discovered that "if we build it, they will come" has as much to do with passion as with presence. They learned the hard way that brand reputation only goes so far.

I met with Ernesto Hernandez, one of the players in this story, in the corporate offices of General Motors Mexico City. I found him to be a soft-spoken yet commanding presence with a sense of humor and strong intelligence.[3] His office looks out at an architectural splendor, Museo Soumaya, a giant, silver, glittering building that curves its way upward like a whale's tail touching the sky. Hernandez shared this view and then quickly got down to the business at hand, discussing the creation of a manufacturing facility. I was ready for a story full

Behind the Scenes: Olga Oro Makes an Introduction

I met Olga Oro for the first time at a conference in Mexico City. Little did I know she was the reason I was invited to the conference to speak. Oro had read my first book, *Follow the Other Hand*, and then passed it along to the owner of the event with a recommendation to engage me. She is like that. She meets someone she likes or admires and wants to share that person with others. My Assumpt! is that Olga Oro was a matchmaker in an earlier life. So it was no surprise when she asked me if I would like to interview President and Managing Director of General Motors Mexico, Ernesto Hernandez.

of "corporate speak" but instead walked away with a very personal one illustrating that even when you have the full support of a global organization, there are times when you feel completely alone. These kinds of circumstances will challenge, on a very personal level, many of your core assumptions about what drives success.

In 1994, Hernandez and eight of his peers were asked to build a manufacturing plant. Each member wore a different hat, and Hernandez at the time was the engineer. Others were in HR, purchasing, logistics, plant management, etc. Hernandez and his team were tasked with creating a General Motors plant in Silao, Mexico, but it needed to be in secrecy, as GM would be phasing out another active plant in Mexico City. The Silao location was chosen because it was equal distance between the Pacific and Atlantic Oceans and the US border and tip of Mexico. This strategic placement combined with the Fair Trade Agreement made shipping the product from this location very cost-efficient. But little did they know, in taking on this massive project, Hernandez and his team would be dropped in a barren land.

The Silao location had no water supply, no workforce, and no roads to support employees coming to the facility. While the location made sense logistically, nothing else did. What Hernandez remembers in the way of a welcome were the thousands of insects that descended upon them and swarmed and darkened the skies. It was at this point that they recognized this was anything but a "build it, they will come" scenario, even though GM is one of the largest employers in the United States and Mexico.

What It Takes to Make the Dream Come True

Hernandez and the team assumed that talent wouldn't be an issue as the state of Guanajuato, where Silao sat, had a growing number of potential employees who worked in other industries but whose talents could be transferred to manufacturing. So all they had to do was set up operations and "they would come." After all, GM is big, and what they had to offer was new and attractive to the area.

Yet they couldn't attract talent because there were no roads to get there. Then, when the roads were built, they couldn't attract a workforce because there were no buses to get to the site.

And eventually, when they could offer buses, the people were too far away to come. And there were no homes, schools, hospitals, restaurants, or football fields for the workforce to stay.

Even though they had full support from GM in Mexico City just two hours away and GM headquarters in Detroit just four hours away by plane, they were alone. But alone together.

In the end it wasn't cement, metal, nuts and bolts, or a corporate name that built the plant. It was the ability to adapt and change and take little for granted. For example, they needed to develop innovative methods for recruiting. Once they found the people, Hernandez and his team had to become creative in how they selected the talent. The point is they were constantly forced to keep doing things differently.

The GM team moved their homes to this barren countryside to create their own community. There was no commuting as they lived and worked in a makeshift town. They had many dreams of how to lay out the plant and ideas for building engines, creating towns, and manufacturing methods. However, these dreams and ideas were often short-lived as the costs for doing them made them unrealistic. But the team's passion to create a great plant and think differently never floundered. They continued to challenge their assumptions around what a big brand can do versus what they needed to do.

Tools: Separating Dreams from Reality

• **Challenging the assumption that we are GM and "we can do it all."** Hernandez and his team quickly began to evaluate their strengths and recognize their limitations. This helped them realize that they couldn't do it all. Instead of trying to build their own community and city infrastructure, they sought the support of the government, citing the plant's ability to increase employment.

• **Challenging the assumption that "we have to have the latest."** When creating something new, it's often enticing to focus on the latest innovations being used by your competitors and assume that is the way to move ahead. The GM teams challenged their assumptions that sometimes the newest way of doing something, such as a sophisticated technique for marrying a chassis to a body, isn't the smartest way of doing it if it's too costly. So they disciplined themselves to stay on budget and at the same time planned to incorporate the latest innovations when the timing and budget were right.

• **Challenging the assumption that "logic always wins out."** Many of the team were technicians and specially trained to think logically and empirically. But in the beginning, many issues required more discussion than what 2 + 2 = 4-type thinking could solve. Thus, emotions at times ran high, but knowing they were in this together with a shared vision held them together.

Passion Attracts as Much as Brand

Within a few months, the team of 9 grew to 100 and then 1,000. Within less than twenty-four months, the first product rolled out the door. In ten years, the plant went from producing engines for trucks to the trucks themselves. And in 2013, GM invested $349 million in expanding the Silao plant.[4]

Before the arrival of Hernandez and his team, Silao was a small agricultural community. Now, it is an internationally recognized industrial conurbation with schools, hospitals, cultural centers, and, of course, football fields. The GM brand is seen as the catalyst for this change.

At the time of this writing, Ernesto Hernandez is now President and Managing Director of General Motors Mexico and the first to point out there is no "father" for this project; he was just one of the people responsible for the Silao plant's success. And as much as he understands the power of the GM brand, he also understands that something looking good on paper or appearing to be a "no- brainer" are just assumptions until put to the test.

Would Hernandez take on this kind of project again? He candidly admitted that much of the time things felt completely out of control. It was not an easy time. Yet, it was an exciting time of challenging assumptions. You can still hear the passion in his voice.

CHAPTER 14

Yeah. Yeah. Yeah.

Comprehending what someone is saying requires the ability to listen, understand, and internalize what is being said. This is becoming increasingly challenging as the ever-increasing speed of life in general, and business in particular, makes us less patient in listening and more quick to respond.

What makes this behavior more epidemic is that our overall attention span is declining rapidly to the point at which a goldfish can hold its focus longer than us.

This chapter is about helping flag the times you are assuming you are listening but, in reality, are not giving yourself the opportunity to digest what is being said.

I have noticed a recent trend of people saying, "Yeah. Yeah. Yeah." These words have different meanings depending on how they are used. Sometimes, they are said sarcastically—for example, when you give an excuse for not getting a job done on time and the other person responds with, "Yeah. Yeah. Yeah. I have heard that one before."

This sort of thing has probably been going on since the first caveman sketched his (exaggerated) hunting exploits on the wall.

The more troubling thing to me is when the words are used to indicate that you understand what is being said—for example, when someone is giving you feedback on something you just did and you say, "Yeah. Yeah. Yeah. I got it."

You likely have used this phrase yourself. Why? Perhaps you felt the need to respond quickly before the other person finished talking? Maybe you felt confident in knowing what the person was thinking and wanted to move on? Maybe you were anxious to insert your thoughts in response to what was being said? Regardless of why you said, "yeah," chances are you were making an assumption that you understood what was being said, even if the thought being expressed to you wasn't complete.

Let's take a look at two ways this assumption articulates itself and how to challenge it when it happens.

The Compulsion to Immediately Supply an Answer

Stephen R. Covey, author of the best-selling *The 7 Habits of Highly Effective People: Powerful Lessons in Personal Change,* observed that "most people do not listen with the intent to understand; they listen with the intent to reply."[1]

I have been guilty of this myself and shared a very personal example at a TEDx talk given at The New York Times building. The story began with my then seven-year-old son Max asking a question.

"Dad, what happens when you and Mom die"?

We were on our way to Max's pool lesson. A year earlier, he had suddenly expressed an interest in learning how to shoot pool. As a parent, when a child expresses an interest in something, you do your best to accommodate with the assumption that it serves as a building block that will translate into professional excellence—in this case, becoming a world-famous pool champion. (LOL.)

Luckily, there was a pool hall two blocks from our apartment in

NYC and the teacher, Tony Robles, loved to teach kids. He was also ranked one of the top-ten pool players in the United States.

Twice a week, Max and I would grab our pool sticks and walk up a busy Manhattan avenue to Max's lesson. It was on one of those walks that Max asked me the question about "death."

Physically, I froze.

Early in the book, I discussed that thoughts are invisible. So to the person who walked around me as I stood motionless, I was just a father with his younger son in the middle of a street as we stared at each other in silence.

Inside, though, my brain was screaming with questions. "Did he see something on TV?" I thought. "Did they discuss this at Sunday School?" I added. "Did one of his friends' parents pass away?" I wondered.

Then, a million possible answers flooded my brain. Little did I realize that the driver behind these thoughts was an assumption: I have to find the perfect answer for Max, and I must find it *now*.

All of this thinking happened within seconds until I finally found my response. But, before blurting it out, I changed tactics. And what happened next was totally unexpected and something I never would have predicted as an answer.

Instead of *answering* the question, I *asked* a question: "Max, why are you wondering about this?"

He didn't hesitate with his answer. "I want to know what happens when you and Mom die," he said, "because I want to know if I get the apartment."

Then, without missing a beat, he added, "because I want to put a pool table in the living room."

I share this episode in my TEDx talk and in my seminars because it underlines how often we feel compelled to reply quickly without really understanding the question being asked. As Covey suggested, this is part of our nature. But in this on-demand world, the compulsion to do things immediately makes this behavior even more dangerous because you don't allow yourself time to digest the content of a question or conversation.

The assumption that you need to respond "now" undermines your ability to effectively manage problems and often sends you in directions that waste time.

A workshop participant shared a story about a new client who had a question regarding the recent installation of new equipment and thus requested a call. The sales manager, who got this message after business hours, panicked because she figured the question had to do with a problem.

Assuming disaster, the sales manager checked back with her team, grilling them on what might have gone wrong and racking their brains on how they could fix what they guessed was the issue. She then spent a night of anxiety waiting for what the client had to say.

In the morning, she reached the client who shared his question: Can they increase their order since everything had gone so well?

Misreading questions goes on in business everyday. How many questions are you asked to answer on a daily basis? "How about if we include this person on the email"? "Should we offer them more money to buy their service"? "Is this the right wording to use in the proposal"? "Why don't we add another person to the team"? "Does this software make sense to use"? The list is endless.

Even though those questions seem clear, how well do you understand what is truly being asked? How often do you take the time to repeat the question before responding to ensure that you are in alignment? How often are you ready to supply an answer or response before you truly grasp the question?

In other words, how often when someone is talking do you think to yourself something like, "Yeah. Yeah. Yeah. I get it. Now let's move on."?

Here is a specific example. I had just finished giving a presentation to the board of directors of a very powerful organization. The women on the board represented some of the most influential CEOs and managers of a retail industry.

The presentation was a hit, and as I was leaving, one of the members asked me if I facilitate meetings. To this day, I regret my answer. "No," I replied as I didn't consider myself a facilitator at the time and assumed she needed an immediate answer. So I followed my assumptions and paid the price. It was the wrong answer for two reasons: people don't like it when you say no, and I had no idea why she asked the question. Her interpretation of "facilitator" could have been completely different than mine. But I will never know. In essence, I had abruptly cut off the dialogue that would have opened doors instead of building a wall.

When people ask a question, it is so easy to allow your immediate assumptions to drive the answer.

When we get up in the morning and our partners or spouses ask, "What's the weather like?" do they really want to know the climate details or information that will help them decide what to wear that day?

When businesspersons of power say they like something and then ask whether you agree, are they looking for your opinion or just confirmation of their judgment?

Making the connection between a question about death and wanting to put a pool table in the living room wasn't obvious. But taking the time to pause and challenge that question wasn't that difficult.

The next time someone asks you a question that demands an important response, don't respond immediately. Turn your assumptions into Assumpts! Then, challenge them so you can explore the question from different perspectives. This acts as a way to press the pause button before responding and allows alternative ideas to appear.

Let me give you an example. Often, a client will ask how quickly you can deliver a product or service. A typical assumption is to respond with a time frame. You assume the client wants it quickly, so you offer a time period that sounds attractive but will be hard to deliver and puts added stress on your team who are already stressed out.

Yet if you recognize your assumption and turn it into an Assumpt!, you might respond by asking things like, "When do you need it?" or "How important is timing for this order?" or "Is time your top priority?" These types of questions enhance the dialogue and exploration. And through it, you learn what is really important to the client rather than just focusing on the surface of that question.

The Danger of Finishing Someone's Thoughts

A 2015 Microsoft research report simply titled *Attention Spans* suggested that the average attention span has shrunk from twelve seconds in 2000 to eight seconds as of 2013.[2] A 30 percent drop is as disturbing as the fact that our ability to focus on a moment is now less than that of a goldfish, which Microsoft reported as nine seconds.

This may explain why you hear so many people finishing other people's sentences by saying, "Yeah. Yeah. Yeah." They are losing focus with what is being said and want to move on, even if it turns out they don't truly understand what is being said.

For example, as the seasons change, I say that "I saw a robin in the tree the other day, and it looks like . . . " And you say, "Yeah. Yeah.

Yeah." and assume I am saying, "it looks like spring is around the corner." But what if I said, "it looks like it's really sick"; or "it looks like a robin, but it could have been a different bird"; or "it looks like it was looking for a worm by tilting its head"?

How often do you unintentionally cut someone off from the conversation with a "Yeah. Yeah. Yeah." (or something similar) because you assume you know what the person is going to say? When you hear yourself thinking or saying these types of words, consider them a cue that an assumption is being made.

Cues You Are Assuming You Understand
What Is Being Said

The sayings below can reflect that you understand what is being said. But if they come the second after the other person finishes a sentence or are said before the person finishes a thought, then the odds are an assumption is in play:

"I get it"!
"Got it."
"Yeah. Yeah. Yeah."
"I'll get right on it."
"I understand completely."
"I hear you."
"Don't worry. I am on top of it."

"I Get It"

Acting as if you don't immediately "get it!" takes a bit of discipline and even annoys people because many see it as questioning the clarity of their directions or statements. My Assumpt! is that people just don't like being slowed down or having to explain themselves. The carpenter's adage of "measure twice, cut once" has little relevance to many. And for practical reasons.

In the software industry, there is a push to fail fast and release early in order to learn, in the real world, what works and what doesn't. Advances in technology have made making a mistake less costly and easier to correct.

For example, I was working with a film editor on a documentary film. Over the course of the project, I kept receiving edits that were not completely thought out. It was as if the editor focused on solving one key problem but not another. Then, when I would point this out, the individual would solve that problem but not others, and the edit still wasn't to my satisfaction. So I spoke to another film editor about this, and he told me "the technology makes it real inexpensive to get an edit out quickly, even if it's not 100 percent right, and then to redo it." He said that it's better to get it wrong four times than spend the time making the first edit right.

Getting a product or service to market quickly is also a competitive strategy. In this strategy, the focus on 100 percent quality takes a backseat because it's not practical to wait until everything is perfect.

My Assumpt! is that this "reality" trickles down into listening. Perhaps it's not as efficient to take the time to truly understand someone's meaning as it is to keep the pace moving?

It is an arguable position. But you have to ask if the potential costs—in creating confusion and getting things wrong—is worth whatever speed is gained.

Tool: Did You Hear What I Just Said?

Overall, I like my phone carrier. Its coverage is great everywhere I go except when I am in my office. Tall buildings cut off my reception there, so I am dependent on using my office Wi-Fi. But periodically, and for no reason, conversations on my smartphone just drop out. People on the other end can hear me, but I can't hear them. This happened so often that I made an appointment at the Apple Genius Bar to have the hardware checked out. It turned out that everything was fine with my iPhone, so the next step was to discuss this with the carrier.

It took about forty minutes to actually connect with a real person as the carrier was updating its systems. When I finally got through, I explained that this was a "service reception" issue, not an iPhone device issue.

But, instead of bothering to understand the problem, the service representative routed me to an iPhone specialist who didn't deal with signal but rather hardware issues. My Assumpt! is that the AT&T representative heard "iPhone" and just assumed that was the issue. This cost me more than an hour of time on the phone and left me with no results but significant frustration.

Sadly, I am seeing this automatic response more frequently across many service companies. Rather than take the time to understand the question, the representatives listen for key words that formulate their response even if it has nothing to do with the question. My Assumpt! is that this is a function of training representatives to work off scripts and to enter key words that generate a verbal response. This is a lot less expensive than actually training the representative to understand the context of a question and then think before responding.

In business meetings, people tend to shy away from asking the leader for clarification. This reluctance is dangerous. It usually traps group members in their assumptions and misunderstandings. After a meeting, have you ever asked colleagues to explain what the boss discussed, and they admitted they had no idea? Have you ever found their interpretation of the discussion to be completely different than yours?

A funny story will underscore this point. I once spoke at a direct marketing conference in Hamburg, Germany. After my presentation, I was invited to listen to the rest of the German speakers. One presenter, a professor, sat at a desk and spoke for an hour and a half with no slides or visual supports. Even with an excellent translator, I couldn't make sense of what he was saying and had trouble staying awake. I kept wondering what I was missing.

At a party after the event, I asked a few of the German participants which speakers they liked the best. "The professor," every one of them replied. "He was great." When I asked them to explain what he said, they responded, "We have no idea. That's what makes him so fantastic!"

As a policy, in both business and in my personal life, I ask people to repeat back what I just said. Admittedly, this practice can annoy the other person, who often feels insulted by the question or frustrated by having to repeat the words. But so often what is repeated back is not what I said, which provides a framework for continuing the dialogue so that we are all in alignment. The individual may be annoyed at having to reiterate the conversation, but it saves him or her from wasting energy by moving forward in the wrong direction. And that saves everyone a lot of frustration.

CHAPTER 15

A Test to Send You on Your Way

Lecturing to thousands of executives and students has taught me that people interpret what you say in many different ways, even when they hear the same thing at exactly the same time. Your experience in reading this book is no different. You will walk away with an understanding that may be different than what I was trying to convey. There is nothing wrong with that. In fact, many times I learn more about a concept that I have taught by listening to what others tell me about what they have learned. Still, there are a few takeaways that I would like all of us to be in alignment with. So I leave you with this brief test.

I invite you to take a simple test. Please indicate if the statements below are True or False:

A. You shouldn't assume.

B. I am aware of most of the assumptions I make.

C. An Assumpt! is the act of acknowledging your assumptions in order to make better decisions and drive innovative ideas.

D. I can manage my Assumpts! to my advantage.

E. All Assumpts! need to be challenged.

F. Once I decide to check my Assumpt!, there are multiple ways to challenge it.

G. I can change my reality by challenging my Assumpts!

The answers to the questions above are below. I trust you got most of them right. If so, you now have a discipline for managing your assumptions that you did not have before. You are on your way to making better decisions because you have enhanced your ability to see things for what they are and are not. You have learned to identify your assumptions and turn them into Assumpts! The purpose of the Assumpt! is to provide you with the power to have better control over your reality instead of letting your assumptions determine your reality.

You also have an effective strategy and tool set for thinking differently. Challenging your Assumpts! breaks through the barriers that are standing in the way of your success in business and in life because it shifts your perspective, providing options, ideas, and innovations that were elusive just a moment before.

It takes time to become sensitized to the process. I have shared many personal stories in this book, illustrating that even someone like me who preaches the importance of identifying and managing assumptions still stumbles. But I have also learned firsthand that I have been able to spot many dangerous assumptions before they injected their potential "poison" in disrupting a new business strategy, relationship, or the writing of this book. The rewards of being able to spot these dangerous assumptions and turn them into allies that drive new thinking or open new doors are intoxicating.

I can't wait for you to experience this yourself. My Assumpt! is that you already have, discovering a new way to change your world, one assumption at a time.

Answers to the Test Above: A-F; B-F; C-T; D-T; E-F; F-T; G-T.

APPENDIX A

Dangerous Assumptions Database (DAD): Your Assumpt! Cheat Sheet

"How do I know I am making an assumption if most of my assumptions are subconscious and taken for granted"? This is a common and crucial question. I have discovered that verbal cues are an effective way to surface your subconscious and enhance the receptivity of your assumption antennas.

The Dangerous Assumptions Database (DAD) was created to help you quickly identify those underlying assumptions acting as barriers to the goals and objectives you are trying to reach. If assumptions are the "mother of all screw-ups," then DAD is at your disposal to aid in quickly spotting these assumptions.

This database was generated by a wide range of business experts, including CEOs from global brands, senior leaders from midsized companies, small business owners, and academics. These individuals represent a wide range of businesses from finance and technology to pharmaceuticals and packaged goods.

Below is a partial list of the key assumptions based on business categories. I propose you glance at them and pay attention to those that resonate. This is the first step toward bringing you closer to recognizing your assumptions.

Then, I suggest the old-fashioned technique of making copies of this section and keeping that copy near your desk. Whenever you feel you have hit a wall, run into a conflict with an employee, or need answers for a situation, scan down the DAD or go to the category that best fits your situation.

You can also go to the home page of andycohen.com to sign up to receive additional dangerous assumptions or to assumpt.com to contribute one of your own assumptions not in the database.

The more you tap into the Dangerous Assumptions Database and practice identifying your assumptions, the greater your leverage in managing your Assumpts!, thinking differently, and making better decisions. Here's the list, sorted by category:

Competition

We will always control the marketplace.

We are the smartest of all our competitors.

If it could be done, our competitors would have already done it.

We're unique. No one is like us.

I know who my competition is.

We don't have the resources to take on the big guy in the category.

We will always be a secondary player in this market.

Consumer Behavior and Demand

Everyone will want one.

Our system is easy to use.

We can just add features to keep clients happy.

Consumers need "us."

Consumers recognize the superior quality of our product.

The consumer is just like me.

Marketing and Sales

We tried it last year, and it didn't work.

The client will never buy it.

Marketing (or Sales) isn't giving me the support I need.

I am the one who drives the revenue for this company.

I have a clear understanding of who the decision-maker is.

It's only a percentage game (volume is more important than quality).

They are idiots if they don't get the concept.

We'll worry about the details later.

I understand my target audience completely.

They'll fill in the blanks.

Our customers are not online.

It's easier to sell products than services.

Leadership and Management

I seem to be the only one worrying about the issues.

If I don't make a decision, then it won't be my fault.

When I speak, my team listens.

My team and my clients make decisions rationally.

The strategy is clear to me. It's my teams who don't get it.

I did your job back when it was "really hard," so I understand how you feel.

I am right. So thanks for your input, but please get it done.

No one lasts more than X years in this position, so it's best not to make waves.

I have to put right my predecessor's legacy and cost-cut excesses before I can even think about how to grow the business.

I can't admit I don't know or have the answer.

No one is watching my actions, so I don't need to walk the talk.

I am not accountable to anyone but my shareholders.

People say what they mean. He didn't say anything, so he's not interested.

I can't tell the truth; it's a career-killer.

We can't delegate real authority, or staff will give away too much.

They will have done their research.

I always do the "right thing." It's the other groups that are messing things up.

My clients (or boss) will never buy this new idea.

Being seen as working hard will make up for not being innovative.

We need to move this through quickly (quickly as defined by the CEO's perceived need, not necessarily by the market or situational need).

It's too late to check with my board or team on my decision.

The reason it's not getting done is stupid.

Someone is taking care of it.

I am too unique or valuable to be replaced.

Because I've committed, they are committed as well.

Streamlining means "cutting costs."

Upper management keeps telling me to change, but they're not leading the change themselves.

There is no reward for doing things differently.

The penalties for taking risks are too extreme. It's easier to sit this out and see what happens.

Failure

If I fail, I will lose my job.

I am going to be judged every step of the way.

There's no difference between a small or large failure. All failures are the same.

How can I make a decision if I don't have all the facts?

Let someone else make the decision and be wrong.

The more I know, the less chance I have of failing.

I am not going to stick my neck out until or unless my superiors do.

A public failure in my organization will haunt my career forever.

Customer Experience

This product is a no-brainer.

The consumer won't complain as long as it's free.

Niche is the key.

A brand extension will be easier to launch than an entirely new brand.

Launching this new product will not cannibalize our existing products.

We can launch this new product using our existing resources and with only a minimal investment in new staff.

Public Relations

Getting "ink" (coverage) is the primary goal of public relations. If I get written up in *The New York Times* or other well-known publications, we'll have it made.

Any type of coverage is more important than staying consistent.

We can generate sales with just public relations.

We don't need to include strategic positioning in our press releases; we just need to offer our products or services.

We don't "really" have competition. There is no one like us.

The effects of PR are instant and are a function of one or two articles.

Our spokesperson or founder always stays on message.

IT and Technology

When I run my software program through a compiler, the outcome is good because the input code was good.

Customers aren't using that technology, so we don't have to care about it.

What my computer is telling me is good information, so there's no reason to question it.

Customers are so enamored with our technology that they will learn all our arcane and obscure procedures and rules.

If they can't understand the directions, then they shouldn't be using the technology.

We have to have these (complicated, arcane, specialized) features to compete.

This feature will make our customers ignore the competition.

If I can't visualize it, then it's not a possibility.

This is the way I use the product, so customers will or should also.

Start-Ups

This will remain true for twenty years.

Because it's in my plan, I have control over it.

All these numbers add up, and there are no errors in the spreadsheets.

This is a "no-brainer."

Everyone on the team is aligned in our vision and strategy.

Compliance

I am not the problem.

This is the way they said to do it.

There's no time to be fully engaged.

Too many rules are killing my revenue.

I follow the rules. It's the other person who doesn't.

This isn't going to hurt anyone.

The lawyers said this is technically legal, so we can't get in trouble by doing it.

Other people are doing the same thing that we propose to do and are getting away with it. We're dopes if we don't follow suit.

Pricing

It costs (this much) to make it. Period.

Customers all understand that a reasonable profit is important.

It costs too much to follow the rules.

People will only value something if they pay for it (versus getting it for free).

Consumers understand our pricing structure, so they will notice if we put in place a new program that isn't 100 percent consistent and logical.

Pricing is too damn complicated—nobody understands how it affects customer behavior.

ENDNOTES

Chapter 1

[1] "Ron Meyer Speaks at TFT Commencement 2012," YouTube video, 16:02, posted by tftucla, June 18, 2012, https://www.youtube.com/watch?v=Vkhn88V_4MM

[2] "Where Is Netflix Available?" Netflix Help Center, https://help.netflix.com/en/node/14164

[3] Shelby Carpenter, "Netflix Is Coming to Comcast Cable TV, and It's a Really Big Deal," *Forbes*, July 5, 2016, http://www.forbes.com/sites/shelbycarpenter/2016/07/05/netflix-is-coming-to-comcast-cable-tv-and-its-a-really-big-deal/#545735bf2e77

Chapter 2

[1] "Mars Climate Orbiter Fact Sheet," mars.nasa.gov, http://mars.nasa.gov/msp98/orbiter/fact.html

[2] Ibid.

[3] Ibid.

[4] Rob Coppinger, "Huge Mars Colony Eyed by SpaceX Founder Elon Musk," Space.com, November 23, 2012, http://www.space.com/18596-mars-colony-spacex-elon-musk.html

[5] Ross Andersen, "Exodus," *Aeon*, September 30, 2014, https://aeon.co/essays/elon-musk-puts-his-case-for-a-multi-planet-civilisation

[6] "My Strife in Court," *The Odd Couple*, writers Neil Simon (play), Jerry Belson and Garry Marshall (developed for television by), Lowell Ganz and Mark Rothman (written by), aired February 16,

1973, http://www.imdb.com/title/tt0664250/; *The 100 Greatest TV Quotes & Catchphrases*, Documentary, TV Mini-Series, writer Gary Simson, 2006, http://www.imdb.com/title/tt0926227/fullcredits?ref_=tt_ov_st_sm. (Lowell Ganz credits Jerry Belson with catchphrase "Never assume, because when you ASSUME, you make an ASS of U and ME.")

Chapter 3

[1] Jill Anderson, "Remembering Professor Chris Argyris," Harvard Graduate School of Education, November 22, 2013, http://www.gse.harvard.edu/news/13/11/remembering-professor-chris-argyris

[2] Peter M. Senge et al., *The Fifth Discipline Fieldbook: Strategies and Tools for Building a Learning Organization* (Crown Business, 1994), 243.

[3] Scott E. Strenger, in discussion with the author, New York City, May 10, 2016.

[4] Ibid.

Chapter 4

[1] Christopher Frayling, *Ken Adam: The Art of Production Design* (Faber & Faber, 2006), 93–100.

[2] Moviefone Staff, "25 Things You Didn't Know About 'Dr. No,' the First James Bond Movie," Moviefone, October 5, 2012, http://www.moviefone.com/2012/10/05/25-things-you-didnt-know-about-dr-no/

[3] *"Dr. No,"* Classic Movie Hub, http://www.classicmoviehub.com/facts-and-trivia/film/dr-no-1962/page/2/

[4] "James Bond: *Dr. No* (1962)," Yarn, https://www.getyarn.io/yarn-clip/f9f38e0d-b9d2-42fc-b707-4247f54c9a4b

[5] *Star Trek II: The Wrath of Khan*, directed by Nicholas Meyer (1982).

[6] *Star Trek*, directed by J. J. Abrams (2009).

[7] Gregory Conti and James Caroland, "Embracing the Kobayashi Maru: Why You Should Teach Your Students to Cheat," *IEEE Security and Privacy* 9, no. 4 (July/August 2011): 48–51, doi:10.1109/MSP.2011.80

[8] Ibid.

[9] Ibid.

[10] Ibid.

[11] "The Top 20 Things Oprah Knows for Sure," Oprah.com, April 14, 2011, http://www.oprah.com/spirit/The-Top-20-Things-Oprah-Knows-for-Sure

Chapter 5

[1] Bill Mason, General Manager of WCHE 1520 AM, radio interview with author, March 3, 2016.

[2] "BlackBerry's Spectacular Decline," Tech Blog, Pingdom.com, September 25, 2012, http://royal.pingdom.com/2012/09/25/blackberry-spectacular-decline/

Chapter 6

[1] "Groopman: The Doctor's In, but Is He Listening?" NPR.org, March 16, 2007, http://www.npr.org/2007/03/16/8946558/groopman-the-doctors-in-but-is-he-listening

[2] Lawrence E. Williams and John A. Bargh, "Experiencing Physical Warmth Promotes Interpersonal Warmth," *Science* 322, no. 5901 (October 24, 2008): 606–607, doi:10.1126/science.1162548

[3] Chunka Mui, "Lessons from Sanjay Jha's Transformation of Motorola," Forbes.com, October 17, 2012, http://www.forbes.com/sites/chunkamui/2012/10/17/lessons-from-sanjay-jhas-transformation-of-motorola/#2e3e23f6352d

[4] Luke Dormehl, "The Oddly Uplifting Story of the Apple Co-founder Who Sold His Stake for $800," Cult of Mac, December 3, 2014, http://www.cultofmac.com/304686/ron-wayne-apple-co-founder/

5 Ibid.

6 Walter Isaacson, *Steve Jobs* (Simon & Schuster, 2011), 66.

7 Peter Densen, MD, "Challenges and Opportunities Facing Medical Education," *Transactions of The American Clinical and Climatological Association* 122 (2011): 48–58, http://www.ncbi. nlm.nih.gov/pmc/articles/PMC3116346/pdf/tacca122000048.pdf

8 Valerie Strauss, "Busting a Myth about Columbus and a Flat Earth," *The Washington Post*, October 10, 2011, https://www. washingtonpost.com/blogs/answer-sheet/post/busting-a-myth-about-columbus-and-a-flat-earth/2011/10/10/gIQAXszQaL_blog. html

9 "Essential Facilitation" (workshop, Interaction Associates).

10 Angela K.-y. Leung et al., "Embodied Metaphors and Creative 'Acts,'" Cornell University ILR School, 2011, http://digitalcommons. ilr.cornell.edu/cgi/viewcontent.cgi?article=1493&context=articles; Suntae Kim, Evan Polman, and Jeffrey Sanchez-Burks, "When Truisms Are True," *The New York Times*, February 25, 2012, http:// www.nytimes.com/2012/02/26/opinion/sunday/when-truisms-are-true.html

Chapter 7

1 John Danner, in discussion with the author, New York City, November 12, 2015.

2 Tom Acitelli, "Turning on the Lite: The Origins of Miller Lite and Light Beer," *All About Beer Magazine*, June 9, 2014, http:// allaboutbeer.com/turning-lite-origins-miller-lite-light-beer/

3 Adam Bernstein, "Joseph Owades Dies at 86; The Father of Light Beer," *The Washington Post*, December 21, 2005, http:// www.washingtonpost.com/wp-dyn/content/article/2005/12/20/ AR2005122001540.html

4 Victor J. Tremblay and Carol Horton Tremblay, "Product and Brand Proliferation," Chapter 6 in *The U.S. Brewing Industry: Data and Economic Analysis* (The MIT Press, 2004), 158.

Chapter 8

[1] Aron Ralston, interview, *Today*, June 4, 2003 (prerecorded), http://www.nbcuniversalarchives.com/nbcuni/clip/5115075415_s22.do

[2] Thomas J. Shimeld, "Harry Houdini's Final Escape," Chapter 5 in *Walter B. Gibson and The Shadow* (McFarland & Company, 2005), 52.

[3] David McCullough, *The Wright Brothers* (Simon & Schuster, 2015).

[4] Adam Grant (presentation at WOBI, World Business Forum, November 17, Lincoln Center, New York City).

[5] Jim Collins, "Building Companies to Last," JimCollins.com, 1995, http://www.jimcollins.com/article_topics/articles/building-companies.html

[6] Tom Clynes, "The Curious Genius of Amar Bose," *Popular Science*, July 15, 2013, http://www.popsci.com/science/article/2013-07/curious-genius-amar-bose

[7] Chad Longell, "Todd Lost Two Legs and an Arm in Afghanistan. That Won't Stop Him from Being an All-American Badass," *Independent Journal Review*, June 2015, http://www.ijreview.com/2015/06/339754-todd-lost-two-legs-and-an-arm-in-afghanistan-that-wont-stop-him-from-being-an-all-american-badass/

[8] "Operation Surf: It Started with a Mission," Amazing Surf Adventures, http://amazingsurfadventures.org/programs/operation-surf/.

[9] Bruce Newman, "Wounded Warriors Ride a Surfboard's Nose, and It Smells Like . . . Victory," *The Mercury News*, April 26, 2012, http://www.mercurynews.com/ci_20489881/wounded-warriors-ride-surfboards-nose-and-it-smells

[10] Tom Clynes, "The Curious Genius of Amar Bose," *Popular Science*, July 15, 2013, http://www.popsci.com/science/article/2013-07/curious-genius-amar-bose

11 "The Bose® Suspension System," Bose, http://worldwide.bose.com/aim/en/web/suspension_system_system/page.html

12 Lance Whitney, "Amazon Third-Party Vendors Sold More Than 12 Billion Items in 2014," CNET, January 5, 2015, http://www.cnet.com/news/amazon-third-party-vendors-sold-more-than-2-billion-items-in-2014/

13 "Passport FAQs" (AGM, May 2007).

14 Rob Stewart, in discussion with the author, May 25, 2011.

15 "Passport FAQs" (AGM, May 2007).

Chapter 9

1 Benjamin Bach, in discussion with the author, January 7, 2015.

2 Mo Costandi, "Synaesthesia—Crossovers in the Senses," *The Guardian,* November 19, 2010, https://www.theguardian.com/science/2010/nov/19/synaesthesia-cross-overs-senses?CMP=twt_fd

3 Beverly D. Flaxington, "Don't Assume I Know What You Mean," *Psychology Today,* October 5, 2012, https://www.psychologytoday.com/blog/understand-other-people/201210/don-t-assume-i-know-what-you-mean

4 Peter Thiel with Blake Masters, *Zero to One: Notes on Startups, or How to Build the Future* (Crown Business, 2014).

Chapter 10

1 Every effort has been made to trace copyright holders and to obtain their permission for the use of copyright material. The author apologizes for any errors or omissions and would be grateful if notified of any corrections that should be incorporated in future reprints or editions of this book.

2 Lee Ann Ghajar, "Wikipedia: Credible Research Source or Not?" TeachingHistory.org, http://teachinghistory.org/digital-classroom/ask-a-digital-historian/23863

3 "John F. Kennedy Speeches: Remarks at the Convocation of the United Negro College Fund, Indianapolis, Indiana, April 12, 1959," John F. Kennedy: Presidential Library and Museum, http://www.jfklibrary.org/Research/Research-Aids/JFK-Speeches/Indianapolis-IN_19590412.aspx

4 http://www.nobelprize.org/nobel_prizes/peace/laureates/2007/gore-lecture_en.html

5 http://www.washingtonpost.com/wp-dyn/content/article/2007/01/18/AR2007011801881.html

Chapter 11

1 Solomon Choi, in discussion with the author, New York City, September 9, 2013.

2 "Our Story," Trader Joe's, http://www.traderjoes.com/our-story.

Chapter 12

1 *Advisory Circular 121–24C Passenger Safety Information Briefing and Briefing Cards* (U.S. Department of Transportation, Federal Aviation Administration, 2013), http://www.faa.gov/documentLibrary/media/Advisory_Circular/AC121-24C.pdf

2 "Funny Steward Southwest Airlines Rapping Safety Information," YouTube video, 2:22, posted by dutchvolvofan, March 18, 2009, https://www.youtube.com/watch?v=pvdCFYLf_JI

3 "Hilarious Southwest Flight Attendant," YouTube video, 3:05, posted by Marty Cobb Smile High Club, April 12, 2014, https://www.youtube.com/watch?v=o7LFBydGjaM

4 "An Unexpected Briefing #airnzhobbit," YouTube video, 4:27, posted by Air New Zealand, https://www.youtube.com/watch?v=cBlRbrB_Gnc

5 Kenneth E. Clow and Karen E. James, "The Marketing Research Process," Chapter 2 in *Essentials of Marketing Research: Putting Research into Practice* (SAGE Publications, 2013), 43.

[6] Dimuth Seneviratne and Brett R. C. Molesworth, "Employing Humour and Celebrities to Manipulate Passengers' Attention to Preflight Safety Briefing Videos in Commercial Aviation," *Safety Science* 75 (2015): 130–135, doi:10.1016/j.ssci.2015.01.006

[7] Ibid.; Dr. Brett Molesworth, "Employing Humour in Pre-Flight Safety Briefings" (conference presentation, 2013).

[8] Dimuth Seneviratne, "Attention during In-Flight Safety Video" (The University of New South Wales, November 27, 2014), http://www.users.on.net/~james.redgrove/APCSWG/SYD2014/UNSW_Attention%20During%20Inflight%20Safety%20Video.pdf

[9] Fong Yee Chan, "Selling Through Entertaining: The Effect of Humour in Television Advertising in Hong Kong," Abstract, *Journal of Marketing Communications* 17, no. 5 (2011): 319–336, doi:10.1080/13527261003729220

[10] "Statistics," PlaneCrashInfo.com, http://www.planecrashinfo.com/cause.htm

[11] Dr. Brett Molesworth, email message to author.

[12] Emily Carrion, "TV Ads and Online Ads Are Better Together," Mixpo, March 6, 2013, https://www.mixpo.com/blog/post/tv_ads_and_online_ads_are_better_together

[13] George Hobica, "What Airlines Won't Tell You during the Safety Demonstration," *The Huffington Post*, last modified May 4, 2013, http://www.huffingtonpost.com/george-hobica/the-things-airlines-dont-_b_2572829.html

[14] Ibid.

[15] http://www.nbcnews.com/business/travel/jetblue-flight-429-hits-turbulence-24-board-taken-hospital-n628941

Chapter 13

[1] *Field of Dreams*, novel by W. P. Kinsella, screenplay by Phil Alden Robinson, Final Draft Screenplay, March 9, 1988, http://www.dailyscript.com/scripts/Field_of_Dreams.pdf

2 Mark Landler, "Wal-Mart Gives Up Germany—Business—
International Herald Tribune," The New York Times, July
28, 2006, http://www.nytimes.com/2006/07/28/business/
worldbusiness/28iht-walmart.2325266.html?_r=0

3 Ernesto Hernandez, in discussion with the author, Mexico City,
April 28, 2014.

4 Thomson Reuters, "GM Is Spending a Lot of Money to Expand
Its Production in Mexico," *Business Insider,* June 27, 2013, http://
www.businessinsider.com/gm-invests-691-million-in-mexico-
plants-2013-6

Chapter 14

1 Stephen R. Covey, *The 7 Habits of Highly Effective People:
Powerful Lessons in Personal Change* (Fireside, 1989).

2 Consumer Insights, Microsoft Canada, *Attention Spans* (Spring
2015), microsoft-attention-spans-research-report-2.pdf

ACKNOWLEDGMENTS

Any creative effort is a sum of its collective parts. Shout-outs to the people who helped me write this book. My everlasting thanks.

Paul Brown for his editorial development, brilliant ideas, and jumping in and righting the ship.

John Danner who first suggested turning the "!" in Assumpt! into a meaningful metaphor.

Val Gelb for her editing skills and ideas for making the writing better.

Julia Gang for her brilliant creativity and cover.

My wife, Deborah Lyons, for her input on the book design.

Mike Ferrell for his graphic designs.

John Ovrutsky, Don Heymann, and Jim Walter for never getting tired of my requests for feedback.

My brother Rich Cohen and my mom, Estelle Cohen, who took the time to listen to my wild ideas and then asked me the tough questions.

Claire Lynch and Sally Bogus for offering to be a sounding board for their uncle's ideas and writing.

James McMahon for his expertise on 007.

Evan Schwartz who began as my writing partner.

Thank you to all the people included in this book who shared their lives, challenges, and achievements.

And kudos to an amazing team that always worked 110 percent in getting this book written and produced:

Cover Design: Julia Gang (juliagang.com)

Interior Design: Robin Krauss (bookformatters.com)

Editing: Andrea Barilla Editing and Writing Services (andreabarilla.com)

Ebook Conversion and Marketing: Brian Schwartz (selfpublish.org)

ABOUT THE AUTHOR

Andy is a popular and recognized TEDx speaker, author, and international thought-leader. He has a degree in experimental psychology and a room full of prestigious advertising awards. Most importantly, he has a track record for helping organizations change the way people think, as measured in millions and millions of dollars in sales. Andy Cohen is the Chief Assumption Officer of Andy Cohen Worldwide, a global advisory firm helping multinational companies think differently and make better decisions. Between engagements, Andy teaches at some of the world's most respected universities including New York, Cornell, and Duke Universities; the Indian School of Business; the Qatar Leadership Center; and the Cheung Kong Graduate School of Business. *Follow the Other Hand*, Andy's first book, was a *New York Times* notable book. It has been translated into multiple languages.

Andy Cohen's Keynotes & Presentations

Author Andy Cohen provides engaging keynotes, interactive workshops, and dynamic online courses that dive into the ideas found in *Challenge Your Assumptions, Change Your World.*

Here are just a few of the Assumpt! Learning Outcomes:

Leadership
• Make better decisions.
• Engage and motivate your team to think and act differently.
• Get people to think strategically, not just tactically.
• Break through barriers that stand in the way of your team's success.

Innovation and Creativity
• Increase your ability to think differently.
• Shift perspectives and change.
• Reengineer your thinking to generate innovative ideas.
• Challenge the assumptions standing in the way of adapting to a new marketplace.

Marketing and Sales
• Enhance creative thinking.
• Turn "No" into "Yes."
• Challenge industry assumptions to differentiate your business from the competition and drive sales.
• Identify the true decision-maker.

Diversity
• Learn how to see things from the other person's perspective.
• Explore the dangerous assumption that what is clear to you is clear to others.
• Learn how to accept other peoples' differences to create a more aligned and inclusive workforce.

**For more information on keynotes and workshops,
visit andycohen.com
or contact andy@andycohen.com.**

CPSIA information can be obtained
at www.ICGtesting.com
Printed in the USA
LVOW10s1437230717

542318LV00012B/759/P

9 781629 670768